EVERY LAST GIRL

Advance Praise for *Every Last Girl*

'Safeena Husain's journey reveals the quiet revolutions unfolding in India's most forgotten corners, where a single woman's courage can tilt the nation towards justice. Her work in bringing back girls into classrooms is not mere service—it is the reclamation of dignity and the shaping of a civilizational future. This book moved me deeply and reminded me that the destiny of our country is written in the dreams of its daughters.'

—BANU MUSHTAQ,
author and activist

'In *Every Last Girl*, Safeena Husain shines a keen and compassionate light on the last girl at the first mile of development. By working closely with the local samaaj—the community—her organization, Educate Girls, has succeeded in creating a societal mission to help these antimbalas become prathambalas, the first girls in their families to be educated. This is how positive, exponential change begins. Do read this book.'

—ROHINI NILEKANI,
chairperson, Rohini Nilekani Philanthropies

EVERY LAST GIRL

A Journey to Educate India's Forgotten Daughters

SAFEENA HUSAIN

HarperCollins *Publishers* India

First published in India by HarperCollins *Publishers* 2026
An imprint HarperCollins *Publishers* India
HarperCollins *Publishers* India, Cyber City, Building 10-A,
Gurugram, Haryana—122002, India
www.harpercollins.co.in

4 6 8 10 9 7 5 3

P-ISBN: 978-93-6569-205-1
E-ISBN: 978-93-6569-789-6

The views and opinions expressed in this book are the author's own and the facts are as reported by her, and the publishers are not in any way liable for the same.

The names of the girls in this book have been changed to protect their privacy and dignity. Some details have been modified to prevent identification.

Typeset in 11.5/16.2 Sabon LT Std
by HarperCollins *Publishers* India Pvt. Ltd

Printed and bound at
Repro India Limited

FSC www.fsc.org MIX Paper | Supporting responsible forestry FSC® C047271

This book is printed on FSC® certified paper
which ensures responsible forest management.

*

HarperCollins Publishers, Macken House, 39/40 Mayor Street Upper,
Dublin 1, D01 C9W8, Ireland

I have never met a girl who said to me,
'You know, I want to stay at home. I want to graze the cattle.
I want to look after my siblings.
I want to be a child bride.'

Every single girl I meet wants to go to school.

Contents

Preface

'India is a land of contrasts,' my father used to say. As a man in the tourism business, his job was to show India to groups of tourists who arrived from all over the world—from the US, the UK, Europe and sometimes as far off as Japan, South Africa or Trinidad. He loved his country and wanted people to not just visit monuments, but really understand its history, people, culture and complexities.

My father would say it is incorrect to think of India simply as a country—it must be viewed as a subcontinent. The country with the highest population and largest democracy in the world, seventh-largest land mass, with twenty-two official languages and hundreds of dialects. 'There is an India for everyone,' he would declare, as if performing on stage.

Here we have a story of innovation and progress. Yet there is also a story of struggle and exclusion—from this let's gallop into the twenty-first century. Now, India has luxurious five-star hotels, and tourism remains a buoyant industry, yet it is also a land where people sleep under plastic sheets. It has the world's biggest middle class and a growing number of billionaires making their money in industries like pharmaceuticals and software—along with one of the highest population of people living below the poverty line.

India stands shoulder to shoulder with only 31 per cent of UN member states that have had a female head of state. Over 150 women were directly or indirectly involved as scientists and engineers in India's space mission to Mars, and we have seen several prominent female chief ministers and leading bankers, including one of the top positions at the Reserve Bank of India. Women can rise to the very top in India and, yet, we remain blighted by low female literacy rates in many parts of the country.

Our education system is also a place of contrast. On one hand, we have some of the world's premier state-funded tertiary education institutes like the Indian Institutes of Technology and Indian Institutes of Management, many of which appear on lists of the world's top fifty institutions. Their alumni are the 'who's who' of the Silicon Valley. On the other, we have one of the largest numbers of out-of-school children in the world.[*1]

This dichotomy can be hard for people to understand. It can feel jarring to outsiders.

While India is rapidly changing and growing, there are still corners of the country where girls' education is a challenge. This book takes you to those far-off corners. It is not to deny or take away from the progress the country has

---

* In India, the category of 'out-of-school' is broadly interpreted. It covers children who live without a school in reach, those who never enrol despite access and those who enrol but fail to attend regularly or eventually drop out.

made since Independence, but instead, I want to shine a light on the areas that we still need to work on. This is a story of concentrations and hotspots in deep rural, remote areas, where girls are still denied their right to an education.

But what about the boys? you may ask. While girls are disproportionately marginalized, there is no denying that boys are out of school too. During the pandemic, I lived in a small village with my family for eight months, teaching tribal children when our schools were closed for two years. I saw first-hand the tremendous challenges that young boys faced as well.

On the first day of class, I asked all the children to draw a picture of how they saw themselves. Kavita drew herself in a flowing Cinderella dress and Vijay drew himself as a stick figure standing next to a red car and a house—he proudly explained his picture to me and told me how he 'knew what it was like to live in a house that had walls' even though he lived in a hut. One of my favourite students, Nitin, drew himself in a clean formal shirt with red buttons, shorts, shoes, neatly combed hair and a tiffin box; 'with lunch and fruits in it', he explained. He saw himself as a man of education and was desperate to seek it.

In class, he was serious and thoughtful. First to arrive and settle down, last to leave. Like a sponge, he wanted to soak in everything we said or did. He could read most letters, but was still struggling to string them together into words. Sometimes, I walked him back to his hut after we finished. A dwelling built so low that you had to bend almost to your waist to be able to enter. I met his mother too. A strong tribal lady who worked as a labourer. Hard labour. She suffered from rheumatoid arthritis and, on some days, would be in debilitating pain.

One day, with no warning, Nitin stopped coming to class. I went by the hut and was told that his mother had gone with a contractor to work on a construction site in Bangalore, hundreds of miles away, and Nitin had been taken by his uncle to work in a coal mine. Hard (child) labour.

Boys face hardships due to poverty too. It really cannot be denied that boys need an education and support as much as girls. I recognize that; in our work with Educate Girls, as we go door to door to find out-of-school girls, we also check for boys. If they have dropped out, we enrol them too. Our foundational learning programme that we run in grades three, four and five in government schools, teaching Hindi, English and math, includes boys too. Our programmes impact and benefit all, but when we design, we keep our eye on the last out-of-school girl, meaning the symbolic Antimbala.

Just like Arjuna in the Mahabharata only saw the eye of the fish when he shot his arrow, we see and design with keeping the out-of-school and most marginalized girl at the centre. No overthinking, no distraction. Our firm belief is that when you design for the most marginalized girl, you benefit all boys and girls, by unleashing the curb-cut effect.

This curb-cut effect was demonstrated beautifully by American civil rights attorney and civil rights advocate Angela Glover Blackwell back in 2017, who also coined the term.[2] It was the disability activists in the 1970s whose actions inspired the idea of creating curb cuts—ramps of concrete that join the pavement to the road, a bridge for mobility of wheelchair users. Simple. But as it turns out, studies showed that they didn't just benefit those with a disability, but also mothers with strollers and delivery men who had to wheel around large crates, people with wheelie suitcases, runners and skateboarders all headed for the curb cut. Girls' education also has that powerful 'curb-cut effect' that helps boys. However, if you don't design through a gender lens, the default option may not work for girls.

This book is born out of my experience and journey of starting and growing Educate Girls. In a world historically designed by and for men, we design for the very last girl, but in doing so design for all. This book is from that gender lens. It focuses on Antimbala, the last girl, and her reality. Women and girls hold up half the sky, and this book is a call to action to not leave any girl behind. We want to see everyone in India thrive and see the country thrive as well. And the good news is, we know how to do this.

But this is not a story of attribution. We have not managed any of the progress we have seen in rural India over the last eighteen years on our own. The Educate Girls movement is just that, a movement powered by funding partners and the government at every stage. I founded Educate Girls back in 2007 with a team of passionate individuals whose own lived experience, coupled with mine, made a huge contribution to our mission. However, this is not limited to my and the teams' effort; as none of this would have been possible without the thirty-plus partnership agreements we have signed over the years with the state governments where we work. The partnership and the championship we have seen from government leaders and bureaucrats gave us the wings we have needed to fly, and the licence and legitimacy to operate.

From my pivotal first meeting with a certain minister for human resource development who gave us our very first partnership in Pali, to our ability in one of our new states to go from zero to a full-fledged technical assistance unit in the government in under three months, the government has walked this path with us. The latter successful partnership was initiated because of a social media post that was picked up by a journalist, who introduced me to the top official at the education ministry who got his team to talk to my team in the space of a twenty-four-hour period. You might challenge this speed, this reality, but sometimes things like this happen, just like this, and government partnership has to be a balance of tenacity and long-term thinking with an impulsive 'seize the day' mentality. Sometimes being in the right place at the right time can help you turn some of the biggest corners in your journey!

And finally, this journey would not have been possible without a relatively modest group of bold funders who have dared to dream big with us and, over the years continued to support our ambitious plan for girls. You know who you are! This group of individuals, with the support of the organizations they run, have invariably all been to Rajasthan, met with our girls, knocked on doors, sat with our teams and truly lived and breathed our work with us. And in doing so they have believed or at times suspended belief as we have taken decisions, and increased the depth and reach of our work, year on year. None of this would have been possible without their support: the fuel, the thought partnership and the trust.

Although we've had a head office in Mumbai since 2008, our work truly happens in India's villages—villages I have visited many times each year throughout our journey. The years often blend into one another, and it is the seasons I remember: the heat of the May sun, the anticipation of the monsoon in the air or the coolness of January mornings. Every year follows a similar cycle: the initial contact with a village and the door-to-door survey, followed by the enrolment campaign, then work in the schools and ongoing visits to families still struggling to enrol their girls.

Most of the stories I'm about to share are from our first five years, largely in Rajasthan. But since 2015, I've met girls across the states of Uttar Pradesh, Madhya Pradesh and Bihar, and even today I continue to uncover stories that sharpen our arguments and illustrate the challenges we—and our girls—still face; stories I feel compelled to share.

I invite you all to join me as we delve into the story of Educate Girls, and it begins like this ...

Introduction

I was lying on a rug in a circle of strangers. A shaman was leaning over me as a waft of intoxicating herb-infused smoke paused by my nose long enough for me to breathe it in and relax even further into the hard ground. She wore an embroidered crimson and white dress and her long, beaded earrings adorned with feathers, like a couple of little dreamcatchers, moved in front of my face hypnotically. I could feel heavy, isolated spots of warmth on my chest and stomach. The hot stones.

'I see you in education!' she whispered close to my ear and then louder to the group. 'She will work in education!'

That was my first and last experience of a healing stone ceremony in Puerto Escondido, Mexico. And it was a prediction that I put out of my head for many, many years. Even when a pushy young journalist met me around six years later, none of this came back to me!

'Why?' the interviewer demanded, somewhat abruptly. 'Why did you decide to work in girls' education?' he asked. It was 2008 and he had come from the local paper, wanting to interview me regarding Educate Girls. We were sitting in our first head office in Oshiwara, Mumbai, barely which was 300 square feet, housed in a small building that faced a slum. As one climbed to the fourth floor, their footsteps echoed up the stairwell almost musically, and the walls were unceremoniously dappled with paan spots. Sometimes you encountered small empty booze bottles and a mound of cigarette butts in the corners. While the building was small, dilapidated and dirty, our office was neat, clean and well lit. Sitting at our tiny four-seater 'conference table' that also doubled up as a place for lunch, I remember being deeply irritated with his question. I tried to tell him that I worked in girls' education because it was an important cause. I tried to nudge him in the direction of how we do our work, telling him about our impact and how it changes girls' lives. He tried to ask me the same thing a few times, but seeing how I was being so evasive, he finally gave up.

Immediately after he left, I remember sitting with my team and expressing my frustration at his persistent questions. Who was he, this assertive young man, in his smart pressed shirt, a pen and a comb peeking out of his top pocket, and a scruffy notebook in his hand, to ask me all these questions? Why was he insisting on knowing this detail? How was it so important to him or to his readers? Why didn't he ask me only about my work? But later, on my way home in the autorickshaw, I reflected on it. I thought more about his probing question. Why did I want to do this work? Why was this mission important to me? More importantly, and perhaps the bigger question, why did I not want to answer these questions? Why was I so irritated and agitated by him? Why was answering a *personal* question so hard?

Looking back now, I think it was still too early for me to articulate it. It was some time later that I was able to admit the personal reason behind my work. And many more years had to pass before I could say it aloud and allow it to be heard. Even today, talking about myself and my own connection to our work is hard, and the conversation always starts with a hard, painful lump in my throat and ends with an overwhelming feeling of shame and vulnerability that makes me want to crawl into bed and hide.

I do this work because of the role education has played in my own life. It took me a long time to gather the courage to say that I grew up around hardship, poverty, violence and abuse. Due to the trauma I experienced as a child, my education was interrupted for three years. How could I begin to describe to an interviewer—a stranger—not just the darkness of my childhood but the three years of self-loathing and failure staring me in the face? Three years of hearing family friends and relatives sympathize with my father and stepmother, saying, 'Poor Yusuf, he is having such a hard time with his daughter.' The hushed tones. The conversations behind closed doors.

Three years is a long time in a teenager's life. Time moves slowly for you whilst it races for your classmates. You remain sitting at home, while they are graduating from university and planning their next steps. Life is moving forward for everyone but you. And so it would have continued, and perhaps even ended in marriage, if I hadn't managed to escape. Marriage, according to my relatives and my father's friends, seemed to be the only route available to me. 'She should settle down.'

But I was very lucky. A family friend stepped in and took me to live with her. She was a beautiful woman from Lucknow, barely four feet eight inches tall, but enormous in heart and compassion. She opened up her home to me, made a place for me in her family and gave me the unconditional love and attention I so clearly craved. She reminded me years later that when I moved in with her, I weighed almost nothing and looked sunken, hollowed out—like death warmed up.

Not only did she fill me up again, with the love and stability I needed, but also gently built my aspiration and confidence to return to the classroom. With that, I got back to education and ended up studying at the London School of Economics (LSE), becoming the first in my family to go overseas for education.

My renewed education trajectory changed my life. People who had written me off, who were so sad for my poor father, suddenly saw me differently. From being the useless daughter, I was now a smart young woman. More than anything, beyond what anyone else thought, I saw myself differently. The day I walked down Houghton Street, past the Wrights Bar and into the Old Building for my first lecture in the New Theatre, I was a changed person. I hated myself a little less, held my head a little higher, began to find my voice and confidence and gained a tonne of experience living independently and studying in London for three years.

After I graduated from LSE, I did not wish to go back to India. I had been thriving away from home. It felt too soon to give that all up and go back to New Delhi. So, I moved as far as I could to the other side of the world, to San Francisco. There I got an entry-level job at a software start-up in 1995 that was making a 3D web browser. But I stayed on the job for less than nine months. I started volunteering for Bay Area nonprofits, and in a short space of time, it was clear that this was where I was meant to be. I ended up working in the social sector within a year of leaving college. It was here that I found my home.

From a volunteer, I moved up to a full-time job to lead a health nonprofit. I scaled their work from one programme in Ecuador to five countries, including Mexico, Bolivia, South Africa and India. It was a heady time for me. I had lived in India all my life except for the time in London for university. This was the decade I explored the world, working in Quito, Cuenca, Manta and deep in the Ecuadorian Amazon jungle with the Shuar tribes of the Pastaza province. I worked in the indigenous areas in Puerto Escondido in Oaxaca Province, in Mexico and in South Africa, spending time in Cape Town and Durban. This was a decade of learning how to build an organization, lead teams, raise funds and understand grassroots work in the most remote and tribal areas in the world.

It was while I was working in Oaxaca that my colleague at that time, Betsy Fuller, and I had been lured to a remote village for that prophetic healing-stone ceremony where the shaman had announced that my future would be in education. Her words had been so confusing to me at the time. I had never thought about education as a career. My own education had been patchy. I had no skills or interest in that area.

Betsy and I laughed all the way back to the town. I regaled her with anecdotes from my childhood. How because of all the challenges at home my report cards always said 'attendance irregular', while I stood first in my class and was a prefect in high school, in fourth grade my rank was twenty-seventh in a class of fifty-plus and how I managed to start university only at the age of twenty-one, where all my classmates were barely eighteen. We laughed off the prophecy as mumbo jumbo and forgot about it until fifteen years later, when Educate Girls was receiving a big award, and I was preparing to go on stage. I was in Oxford to receive the Skoll Award for Social Entrepreneurship. My family were in the audience, my phone was in my pocket and, just before I stepped on stage, I took it out to make sure it was on silent and saw a message from Betsy. 'Good Luck—go for it ... Remember what the shaman said!' reminding me of where it all began.

But as I said after the meeting with the shaman, I had brushed off this idea of working in education and went back to my work in community health and it wasn't until 2004 that something changed. The majority of health centres I visited in my work were located in South America, but on one particular day I found myself back in India for a relatively brief trip. I had landed two days earlier and passed through my native place, New Delhi. During my formative years this sprawling, low-rise city had been my family home, and it was where my father still lived. We hadn't seen each other for a while, and he didn't want to let me out of his sight—I was now his smart, educated daughter, who he was genuinely very proud of. So, I agreed that he could accompany me on my work trip to the mystical foothills of the Himalayas.

We had already been in the car for over eight hours when we reached the outskirts of the village and abandoned the car in order to continue on foot. It was meant to be a typical journey where I was keen to stare aimlessly out of the window and catch up on some sleep. But my father had other plans and grilled me about San Francisco, my work and when I was going to come home!

'Arre Daddy! San Francisco is my home.' I replied. Work is good. Life is good. '*Jaane bhee do!* Let it be!'

The road to the village snaked up the mountain and shortened the travel time to a quarter. The mountain side was overwhelmingly steep and the village was hard to make out as it was hidden in the trees. Only the temple was really visible, with a white steeple, moulded like icing on a cake and an orange flag just above the canopy. As my eyes adjusted to the verdant slope up to the left and stepped agricultural fields back down the hill to our right, I became suddenly aware of punctuating flashes of crimson, magenta and mustard yellow as a group of veiled women in sarees appeared from their houses and approached us along a narrow lane.

Once the group had all arrived, one of the more confident women greeted us with deference. We introduced ourselves, and then she turned and asked my father, somewhat forwardly, how many children he had.

'Here she is. My only child. My everything!' he said, gesturing towards me.

His arms were open and he wore a smile that concealed nothing and revealed everything—pure love and pride. I smiled too. But, on turning back to the women I saw that some of them had started crying. They expressed deep sorrow for my father, as if it was a curse to have a daughter as your only child.

'*Kitana bojh hai!* What a burden!' was their solemn conclusion. You are still young, they told my father, you can try more. A man must have a son, they advised.

I was left with a hollow sadness, and a reminder of the social pressures I had experienced myself as a girl. How can sadness be attached to the life of any child? What had those women experienced themselves as little girls? I asked myself. What pressure were they under in their extended families?

In that very moment, my life changed.

During our visit it was clear that none of the women in the village were literate. Our community clinic was set up with that in mind, in the knowledge that the women who will take all the decisions in their families about their own and their children's health would not be able to read, would have restrictions on their mobility and would likely suffer from a wider range of health issues, linked to poor nutrition, limited access to hygiene and sanitation, and both mental and physical abuse. And why? Well, because they were women. 'Being born female is dangerous for your health' is how my old mentor Anne Firth Murray put it.[1] As a professor at Stanford University and the founder of the Global Fund for Women, she spoke with wisdom and experience.

On the car journey back down the mountain and through the plains back to the capital, I reflected on the fact that I might have been born in that village. It was just a matter of fate that I was born to my mother and my father in New Delhi, rather than a village near Mussoorie. It was fate that I eventually managed to complete my education with the help of my aunt. Why was I living in San Francisco and running a health nonprofit, when these women were not able to read their prescriptions? They were the same age as me. We grew up in the same India. But I was who I was because of my education. They were who they were because they had been denied their education.

That day sowed the seed for Educate Girls. By 2005, I was back in India, choosing Mumbai to make my home and start thinking about my plans. But this journey from Delhi to Mumbai via London and San Francisco was not something I was able to share with the interviewer that day.

It's now been eighteen years since I started Educate Girls, and it has grown from a handful of team members to thousands of full-time employees and tens of thousands of village-based gender champions. In those eighteen years, the team, in partnership with communities and state governments, has mobilized over two million out-of-school girls to bring them back into the classrooms and supported learning outcomes for 2.4 million children, boys and girls.

During these eighteen years, I have stood on the doorsteps of families from tribal communities, sat with girls, met with officials in government education departments, negotiated with data scientists in shiny Silicon Valley offices and addressed crowds on stages in rural towns. I have also experienced and witnessed the impact of gender-based violence, I have been exposed to the reality of what it is like to be born a girl in certain communities in India, knowing that thousands of girls don't survive and aren't even born.

But this is not a problem just of India, it is a global concern. 'Women's rights are human rights. Human rights are women's rights,' Hillary Rodham Clinton declared forcefully in 1995, at the Fourth UN Conference on Women in Beijing,[2] in what is now seen as a watershed moment in the women's rights movement. And this is exactly where we begin this book, as I start to explain why girls' education matters and why it is every girl's right. Why geography and gender are a double jeopardy and why women and girls always come off worse, whether in migration, conflict or climate disasters.

The world is made for the educated, and without an education, you are unlikely to know your rights and are much more likely to be open to exploitation and exclusion. If you live on the margins physically, economically and socially, there is a high likelihood that you will remain uneducated. But more than that, if you are then also born a girl, in a world that is by and large made by and for men, then your life story is invariably written for you. Your story is written for you through a lens of disappointment. Your story is written from a mindset that values a girl less than a boy. It is a mindset that keeps girls out of school, and yet it is school and a quality, gender-transformative education that will ensure that *more* girls are not denied the education that is rightfully theirs. The solution lies in the problem itself. Education begets education.

In this book, I would like to rewrite the story for the girls I have met, and for those I haven't. And through my story and the story of Educate Girls, the organization I founded, I would like to explain why I, and why we *all,* need to educate girls.

This book is about the problem of girls' education, but it is also about the potential of girls' education. By reading it,

I want to give every reader hope and a sense that something human and fundamental like girls' education—that doesn't require any new inventions, doesn't require rocket science—can ensure that we all survive and thrive. We know how to do this, and I can and will explain how. How gender champions are coming forward from the most remote villages, men and women alike. How technology is helping us find hotspots of out-of-school girls that still exist despite huge progress. How data is driving our work and how slowly but surely mindsets and behaviours are shifting, and a movement is being created that will stop at nothing to fight for girls' rights.

We have seventeen Sustainable Development Goals, declared by the United Nations in 2015.[3] But we also have every last girl to find and empower through education. If we do that, those seventeen goals can become one. Our oceans, our health, our forests, our safety, our democratic rights, our ability to survive and thrive: they all become one fight with one solution, which is to educate every last girl. And so, the story shifts to rural Rajasthan.

PART I

Antimbala's World

1

A World for the Educated

UN Declaration of Human Rights, Article 26, 1948[1]

1. Everyone has the right to education. Education shall be free, at least in the elementary and fundamental stages. Elementary education shall be compulsory …
2. Education shall be directed to the full development of the human personality and to the strengthening of respect for human rights and fundamental freedoms ….

'Vibha, do you go to school?' I asked.

'Yes, I do!' the nine-year-old affirmed with a broad grin.

It was early 2008, and while Vibha said she went to school, her name was nowhere to be found in the register. It took some time before I understood what 'going to school' meant to Vibha: a ride to school on the back of her big brother's bike, which she described with glee. She was not registered in the school. She didn't enter the classroom, she didn't have a uniform, books or a bag, she didn't get to study, have playmates, or the hot midday meal, she just enjoyed the odd ride with her brother and on occasions would hang around *near* the school, not *in* the school. Vibha's brother, on the other hand, was in the register. He went to school. Born on the eve of the millennium, Vibha should have been enrolled in 2004 or 2005, but when I met her, she was what the government classified as 'never enrolled'. Her sisters, too, were in the same position. At that time her father, Dinesh Ji, was prepared to enrol his sons in school but not his daughters.

Back then, it was eight years into the new millennium and every girl in India had the constitutional right to go to school. The right exists since 1949, right after Independence, when India drafted its Constitution. Having voted on the Universal Declaration of Human Rights the year before, along with forty-eight other countries, India drew much from what it said. In the aftermath of the horrors of World War II, the UN Declaration called on all governments across the world to protect thirty human rights, including the right to education. And so, as a result, Vibha had a whole host of rights. She had a right to be safe and healthy. She had a right to a voice and freedom of expression. She had the right to play and not work and she had a right to *know her rights*. That knowledge had to come through an education. Vibha had an equal right to an education, but when I met her, just before India's Right to Education (RTE) Act became a law in 2009, she wasn't going to school.

It is all well and good to have a Constitution and protected human rights, but so many rights are impossible to access if you remain without an education. In the sixty years that passed since drafting the Constitution, India had not done enough to ensure its girls were going to school. Constitutional rights existed, but the Constitution lacked real enforcement power. It took a 1997 amendment and, later the 2009 RTE Act, to finally compel the government to guarantee free and compulsory education for all children aged six to fourteen. With the RTE Act, the government was mandated to deliver education, and that meant building schools and hiring and training teachers. It also became mandatory for a parent to send their child to school. A lot changed after 2009, but that was no help to Vibha and many others in 2008. Without school and the ability to read, their world was a distorted place.

I had founded Educate Girls a few months before we met Vibha for the very first time. The mission of the organization was focused on out-of-school girls. Girls who had either never enrolled in school or had been enrolled but then dropped out. This mission was close to my heart as my own education had once been interrupted. During that period in my life, sitting at home, I felt like all my friends had moved ahead in life and there was no future for me—I felt voiceless, trapped and helpless. I blamed myself for not being smart enough and for my failure. The only future people saw for me was marriage and children. Aunties set up matches, saying things like, 'The boy is a divorcee with four children. He will be perfect for her. She can settle down.' However, I was lucky my life found a different path. A path made possible only by education.

With Educate Girls, I started work in the state of Rajasthan, the largest state in India in terms of land mass. Land of the kings, it is the state of lake palaces, pink palaces, blue cities, colourful turbans, the seat of the early maharajas, a home to camels and tigers—today, it is the top location for celebrity destination weddings. Economically, it now survives on tourism, agriculture, textiles and minerals—and yet the population is still overwhelmingly pastoralist.

In 2005, when I returned from San Francisco, while India still felt the same, Mumbai as a city was new to me and felt like a big contrast to Delhi. It took a lot of time to get used to. Everyone was busy and no one cared about where you were from or your background. Almost everyone here was from somewhere else. While it was fast-paced, I found it to be much more relaxed than Delhi. India had definitely changed in the fifteen years I had been away. So much progress had taken place—from advancements in technology, to opportunities for young people and access to the latest fashion, movies and music. Before moving abroad for studies, the only cars we had in India were Ambassadors, Marutis and Contessas. Now cars of all brands were on the streets and big malls with the latest brands were the norm.

But India is not defined by just its cities. Post-liberalization, while Indian cities galloped into the twenty-first century, much of rural India was and still is stuck in another era. The travelling time from Mumbai to Jodhpur has now reduced from eighteen hours by train to just one and a half hours by plane. The skies are criss-crossed with a web of domestic flights, while girls walk beneath the fluffy lattice trails left by the planes, oblivious to the industry in the sky that is commanding 10,000 rupees for a flight, equivalent to more than a month's worth of wages for their mothers. While in the cities, couriers deliver the latest electronic devices home in the blink of an eye, but the villages have no running water, and girls walk miles to collect water in urns.

If you got a pin and stuck it plumb in the very middle of Rajasthan, you would hit the northernmost tip of Pali district. It lies up and over the Aravali mountain range if you drive north-west from Udaipur on the way to Jodhpur, and in just under four hours you are at the foothills that form the eastern boundary of the district. The northern border of the state is essentially the Luni River, an unusually saline river that disappears into the Rann of Kutch, Gujarat's famous salt marshes. The eponymous city of Pali might have a thriving industry, but the landscape is made up of undulating planes and scattered hills and, is for the most part, rural and remote.

It was here that we laid the foundation of our work. In 2007, we established a small office in a village just outside the town of Falna, halfway between Udaipur and Pali city, and I used to travel there from Mumbai on the overnight train, setting my alarm so that I didn't miss the one-minute stop as the train pulled into the town. I would hurtle off the train as it ground to a halt, only to hear the doors clatter shut behind me just as my feet touched the platform and the train screeched off again on its way to Pali and then Jodhpur.

The organization had started working in a number of villages in the district, and in the initial days we held several gatherings to build awareness of our mission and find like-minded people to join us. One of these was held at a hired hall in Falna, the closest town to the office we had just set up. It was a town of contrasts, consisting of the only hotel and cinema for miles, and a bazaar that sold camel-hide juttis and dried desert vegetables. It was a great place to buy local clothing, and it also housed a large temple and a big bus terminal that ensured connectivity across the district. As it turned out, it was also a great place to host a meeting where we wanted a large number of people to attend from nearby villages all over to hear what we had to say.

Upwards of forty-five young people from the surrounding villages arrived for the meeting. The majority of the crowd were young men, but behind them, in the far-right corner of the hall, were six young women. To engage this new audience and a new way of working we started off the day with some storytelling. Staff members began with deeply personal stories of their own experiences with education and oftentimes mentioned the exclusion of either themselves or a female family member from the school system.

I was deeply moved by everyone who spoke, and I started to mentally go over what I would share if I was to stand up and speak. I hadn't shared my personal story before in this context, always leaning into my work experience in community development and my academic credentials rather than realizing that my true qualification to do what we were doing was my own lived experience of struggle for my education and for self-determination. And my own escape from poverty and abuse. Up until that day, I had not been ready to disclose this, but the more stories I heard the more I realized the importance of my own journey. So much of what the others shared resonated with my own experience, but I maintained my 'personal' silence, as I had with the journalist.

After various team members and male guests had spoken, the crowd fell silent, and one of the six women hesitantly stood up from the floor, her crimson saree bunched up in one hand. Her other hand gently pulled back her veil: 'My education is the only thing that is truly mine.' Silence followed. 'No one can beat it out of me. No one can steal it from me. No flood, no famine can take it away; my education will be with me till my dying day.'

Nagina Bano had mesmerized the crowd and me with her impassioned statement. Hearing her was a revelation. And the courage it takes to make yourself vulnerable, to share your story in public. Courage that I could not muster that day or even for years to come. It took a long time for me to be able to tell my own story and not be overcome by shame. I felt that if I shared my story with my team, they would think less of me and not take me seriously. I would not be a strong leader in their eyes. And somewhere they might judge me. It was a fear that haunted me for a very long time. Her courage that day was astounding. In a meeting where there were barely any women, and where the cultural norm was for women to be seen and not heard, she had stood tall.

Nagina had been a child bride, which she told me after the meeting when I went over to speak to her. Her in-laws tortured her and beat her. When she gave birth to a baby girl, she was abused and thrown out of the house. When she failed to give her husband and in-laws their much awaited, much wished-for son, she had no other choice. Unable to go back to her own family because of the shame, she had to start again on her own.

'But there was one thing,' she said, 'I had a little bit of education.' She gestured as if her education could be defined with the space with her finger and thumb. 'So finally, with that, I got a job in the village and I was able to support myself and my daughter.' Her education became her saviour.

Nagina's words have always stayed with me, that 'little bit of education' which turned her life around; she and her daughter had survived because of it. Meeting Nagina was a turning point for me in my understanding of education as a human right, and in my resolve to educate girls. What Nagina said helped me to understand that education is not a gift for us to give. We can't choose who gets an education, and in doing so choose who does not. Education is a human right and a human right is inherent and inalienable. With education, you can advocate for yourself and have the agency to make choices for yourself in the world.

A World through the Prism of Illiteracy

While we know education is a basic right, what we need to really understand is what it means to be *without* an education. What does life look like?

It is very easy to extol the value of going to school through the prism of privilege and literacy. I am who I am today because of my education, an education I too had to struggle to complete. But today, 28 per cent of women in India remain unable to read and write, and in states like Rajasthan the figure is closer to 35 per cent.[2] There is also a big gender gap as more men than women have been able to access their rights. It still shocks me today when I hear our team's stories of the debilitating effect of illiteracy that holds back such a huge number of young women.

The gatherings we held were periods of intense listening which guided us. What were the barriers to going to school?

What were the consequences of remaining illiterate? How did a community really feel about its girls? What was a girl's reality living in a twenty-first-century village in India, in a community that the rest of the country has, to a degree, left behind?

Bhanwari Devi, known to one of our field coordinators, explained her situation to us when we met her during this time. Born into the Meena[3] tribe, she was at the time thirty-two years old and had a family of six to look after. Her husband struggled to get work, so earning a regular income fell on her. Through the government's new MGNREGA (Mahatma Gandhi National Rural Employment Guarantee Act)[4] scheme, launched in 2006, Bhanwari could get work despite lacking an education. The scheme is still the country's largest employer, and, in villages like Bhanwari Devi's, very often the only employer. In a typical month, she should have earned around two thousand rupees for her work planting trees and clearing drains. But as an illiterate woman, she never received the full amount. Just to get her wages, deposit it in the bank and withdraw money when needed, Bhanwari Devi had to pay a fixer at every stage because she herself could not read or write.

Daily wage work through MGNREGA doesn't demand any prior skills or education. Bhanwari actually enjoyed the camaraderie of working with other women in a group. The day started between eight and nine in the morning and there was an hour's break for lunch. The year before she had worked planting trees and was then involved in a drain-clearing project with the same group of women. It was hard work, and gruelling in the summer months. But she enjoyed the labour and being outside. Their MGNREGA Mate (the leader of their group) was an empathetic woman. She had worked for a number of years on the scheme but had been educated up to tenth grade and could therefore take on this supervisory role and support Bhanwari and her team. As they were diligent workers there was rarely a complaint.

The issue for Bhanwari, however, was in accessing her hard-earned wages. The scheme involves payments straight into a worker's bank account. Sensible, of course, but accessing one's own money can be costly when you are not literate. If you are not able to read, you need someone to read for you. If you are not able to write, you need someone to write for you. Even with a guarantee of work, you are not necessarily guaranteed the full wage that is rightfully yours as withdrawals from the bank involve fixers to read, write and help fill the forms that get you what is rightfully yours. These fixers hang around outside banks; they are a permanent 'fixture' and somewhat of a cottage industry—competing for the next 'helpless' (more often than not female) bank client. Those without an education—the poorest community members who the MGNREGA scheme is designed to help—are those who face the highest transaction costs.

This is not an isolated story. Jassi, one of our team members in Pali, witnessed her own mother, Vidya, being exploited in a similar way. Her mother, who had never been to school, was informed by her bank branch that it was closing down and she would need to withdraw all her funds. She was a keen saver and the bank was holding 12,000 rupees of hers—the equivalent of nearly a year's income that she had been putting away, her emergency fund that gave her great comfort in this precarious world. Having been called to the branch by the bank, she made the long journey to the town from her village.

A trip to the town was a financial cost in and of itself: the loss of a day's wages, in addition to the bus fare and the physical toll one had to pay. First there was the walk to the main road. Setting off at 7 a.m. helped avoid the oppressive heat of the sun, but still there was a lick of heat on the crown of her head even at the lowest gradient of its morning ascent. Vidya couldn't read the number on the front, but Jassi had taught her that there was only one bus that halted at her stop, so she could confidently board. It was a high step up, easy to board in a dhoti or jeans, but complicated in a saree, carrying a plastic bag in one hand and holding her veil in place with the other, especially when tired after having walked 3 kilometres already. Juggling all this and hauling herself into the vehicle by way of the rail was an effort, and then there was the fumble for the fare whilst others jostled to get on. She needed three hands. The bus stop was littered with single pinkish-beige or navy-blue plastic slippers that had fallen from people's feet, and these could not be retrieved as people scrambled onto the vehicle. Almost every slipper was a left foot. And this scramble had to be repeated on the way home.

Unable to read, Jassi's mother relied on the bank staff to help her with the form, a procedure she was now used to. On returning home, she explained to Jassi in a resigned tone that, in the end, the bank had given her just 9,000 rupees, as a number of 'charges' had been incurred through the withdrawal process. Unable to read the forms she was signing, let alone the small print, Vidya was not able to avail of the right to her own money. None of these charges were legitimate. This was theft. Jassi struggled to tell me this story, her eyes welled up, and it left me with such a profound feeling of anger at the injustice. Who could a woman trust if she could not read or write?

Another story told to me by one of our block officers left me reeling. When Poonam's husband died at a young age, she was visited in the days after the funeral by her husband's brother and his son, who said they had brought paperwork for her to avail of her widow's pension. Her pension was something she just could not think about at this time. Blinded some days by the grief, living in slow motion, her head was filled with thoughts of her late husband while she wandered around her empty house and stared at her empty bed. She was grateful that someone was thinking about her, as she struggled to think for and of herself.

This is a set of feelings I know only too well. In the days after my father died, right in the middle of the COVID pandemic, I sometimes thought I was in a film, living someone else's life. I was paralysed by grief that came in waves. And when a wave hit, it truly hit. I was reliant upon friends and family to make arrangements, inform people, feed us and support me to make some of the most important and the most trivial decisions. I, too, struggled to think for, and *of*, myself.

So, assuming the paperwork she had been presented with *was* what her relatives said it was, Poonam trustingly signed the forms. She profusely thanked her husband's brother and his son.

The forms were easy to sign, but impossible to read. A few months later, after the expected period of mourning, Poonam left her home to visit her fields. The fog was lifting a little, she was starting to think straight again. But she soon discovered that unbeknown to her, in those grief-ridden days, she had signed her property rights over to her nephew. The forms were not for the widow's pension she had been so grateful for—they were papers pertaining to property ownership. Her gratitude had been badly misplaced. The cruel term 'blind ignorance' comes to mind.

None of these stories are unusual. As we travelled around and listened, we realized the extent of the impact that illiteracy and a lack of education can have on a woman's life. Over half of all women in Rajasthan were illiterate when we started our work. With large numbers of women working under MGNREGA, think of the scale of this vulnerability. The scale of the fraud and exploitation. The scale of the lost wages. The scale of helplessness. The scale of its duration across their lifetimes. The scale and cost of this corruption on individuals, society and our nation.

Educating a Nation

Education is a baseline for nation-building and is taken for granted by most of the world, but if in the twentieth century a majority of your citizens remain illiterate, any national services are incredibly difficult to build. That was the case in Afghanistan, where in 2005, 64 per cent of the male population could not read or write and a staggering 82 per cent of women were illiterate.[5]

I saw this all first-hand in August 2010, when I had the privilege of visiting Afghanistan just after General David Petraeus took charge of the US and NATO forces there. I was there on the invitation of an international development agency, which had been working on a programme to build and equip schools in villages. But every time they completed a school, it was burnt down, usually by the villagers. I was asked to share strategies for building community ownership, as it was clear that the village leadership was highly suspicious of an education agenda driven under a foreign power.

Education had once been highly regarded in Afghanistan. The first girls' school was founded in 1921 by Queen Soraya. In 1978, a million children were in school and Kabul University had a global reputation. However, education in Afghanistan had a chequered history, with the school population rising and falling depending on the state of conflict and the country's leadership, religion and politics.[6]

As we passed through the streets of Kabul in our vehicles, women sat by the side of the road in their signature blue burqas, begging, as half-naked children hurled faeces at our truck. These children were harmless, albeit meting out someone's frustration on us, most likely their parents'. But our protection was extreme. Our vehicles were bulletproof and required two arms to heave the doors shut as they were so cumbersome, and my wonderful chaperone kept her equally heavy helmet on even inside the vehicle. 'I want to live to see my family again!' she told me, somewhat nonchalantly, normalizing the risk. The tension was palpable and the poverty we were seeing was extreme.

She and I shared a container room for a couple of nights, and this wonderful African-American mother of four spoke passionately about her understanding of the situation in Afghanistan while multitasking and checking in on her family back home via video calls. Had they had dinner? And most importantly, had the kids done their homework? Education was everything to her, and while promoting education here on the frontline in Afghanistan, she wasn't going to let it slip on the other side of the world, back home in the US, for her own children!

One story she shared really stayed with me. The task force she was working alongside was training a new Afghan police force to man blockades and look out for suspected insurgents. The success of the blockades and the objective of pulling over certain vehicles relied upon those manning the checkpoints to note down car registration numbers. A simple enough strategy. But the project hit a massive roadblock—forgive the pun—when it was realized that very few of the new Afghan recruits into the police force were literate. As I mentioned earlier, barely 36 per cent of men could read, and the corresponding figure for women was only 18 per cent. Here, improving national security was going to be incredibly difficult without the successful and rapid roll-out of foundational education. The importance of education was clear, but the delivery was challenging. I was very early in the process of scaling up our community-based approach in India and doubted the value I could add there. But the experience was invaluable to me in my understanding of how everything a country does in the aftermath of war is rooted in a solid foundation of education—quick fixes are not going to succeed without an educated nation.

This was as recently as 2010 when a widespread lack of foundational literacy and numeracy in Afghanistan meant that it was proving impossible to recruit a large enough police force from a generation, who had been denied an education. We cannot presume to be able to support communities and nations with peace-building, security and the delivery of basic services if we haven't first fought for and supported the implementation of primary education; education that enables something as simple as the reading and noting down of a number plate. It breaks my heart today to learn that education is being weaponized once again. In 2001, when the Taliban regime fell, not a single girl was in school. Progress was made over the next twenty years, but today Afghanistan is back to being the only country in the world where girls are banned from going to school beyond grade six. Seventy-five per cent of girls are denied education, and the adult literacy rate remains one of the lowest in the world at around 38 per cent. One can only speculate that a lack of education is fuelling this rollback of rights. The Taliban have issued more than a hundred laws that strip away women's rights. Not only have they removed girls' right to education, but they have removed every basic freedom you can think of from employment to healthcare and freedom of speech. To paraphrase Malala Yousafzai, they are presiding over gender apartheid.[7]

Educating a Family

Quality education, combined with an aspirational mindset, has the power to change the trajectory of an individual and a family within a generation. A mirror of this is the case of a wonderful Sikh family I once knew, who left remote rural Punjab to start a new life in the UK back in the late 1950s. The Singhs set up a corner shop in west London, following a well-trodden immigrant path. Their sparky daughters Jasleen and Jasmeet were able to access free, quality education through the UK government's state education system, continuing right up to university where not only was their education offered for free, but they were also able to avail a grant from the government to support their accommodation and living expenses while studying. I met them both at LSE in my second year, where we bonded over our humble roots and shared love of a good party.

We had a fabulous time as desi students together pounding the pavements of Holborn and Covent Garden back in the 1990s. Today, Jasleen works in finance and Jasmeet has created a name for herself as a journalist and documentary filmmaker. They are an incredible examples of how living in a country with good-quality, free public education can fast-track radical changes in a family over just one single generation. Nothing else has the power to accelerate a family's trajectory from running a small corner shop to an international media house or global bank in such a short time.

I see that countries that provide access to quality, free or subsidized education can do this. Not just for nation-building, but for an individual's personal equality and social mobility. A country like Afghanistan is struggling to train a police force. Where will future nurses, doctors, teachers and professors come from without school education for everyone? I am certainly not advocating here for everyone to receive a British or an American education, far from it. The system in both countries is suffering as inequality is on the rise. That said, access to free education is a key, if not the sole ingredient. In the case of my friends, aspiration, parental support and hard work are also big factors as their parents sought better lives for their children. But without quality schooling, such fast generational changes would not be possible. What I am trying to explain is that when every child has an equal opportunity to access free, quality education, it is one of the biggest multipliers and can have an immeasurable impact on the next generation and an individual's life. Free, quality public education is a true equalizer and a protected right. And when that right is not enabled, a whole country can be held back.

When girls are not educated, we pay a heavy price with child marriage,[8] child labour,[9] higher rates of domestic violence, trafficking, low financial inclusion, female labour participation, intergenerational cycles of illiteracy and poverty and high vulnerability of women and girls dying in disasters.

The cost of not acting on this is immeasurable. We pay with unfulfilled dreams and unrealized potential, but mostly a world that remains unjust. In an interconnected and interdependent world, we would be foolish to assume that we can remain untouched and unaffected by that injustice.

The World Today

Education is the key to the empowerment and growth of individuals, societies, nations and to the health of the planet. When in late 2023 Educate Girls turned sixteen, I decided to go back to Pali and visit Vibha to see where life had taken her. We were deep in rural Rajasthan in her village, and as we sat together, the late morning January sun was warm on our faces.

How had life changed for that bubbly, smiling nine-year-old girl, who back in 2008 thought accompanying her brother on the cycle or playing outside the school building was equivalent to going to school? All those years ago we had worked day and night to convince Dinesh, Vibha's father, to enrol her in school. So did she stay enrolled? Did education change her own circumstances and that of her family? Did Dinesh still believe that only boys should be educated?

'My father believes in education now.' Vibha looked over at her father and smiled. 'After I went to a bridge course[10] and then KGBV[11] to complete my tenth, I was able to continue to twelfth and finish school!'

Back in 2008, things were different. Before the RTE Act came fully into force, there was no way for a nine-year-old to enrol in the mainstream primary school after having missed the first four years of education. So the government had launched what were known as bridge courses to deliver an intensive catch-up curriculum and enable children who had never been enrolled to go to school. Vibha recalled with joy her experiences in the course. It was a huge wrench for her and her sisters to be 'sent away' for six months to a residential facility. They missed their parents, but what the course opened up a whole new world to Vibha, one she appreciates so deeply now as she goes about her work. After the bridge course, she and her sister enrolled in the Kasturba Gandhi Balika Vidyalaya (KGBV). The KGBV programme had been initiated by the central government in 2004 to provide residential schools for girls from minority backgrounds, those who were orphaned, whose parents had migrated for work or had difficult circumstances at home. If there wasn't a primary school nearby (which was often the case in remote rural India, before the RTE Act called for an infrastructure drive that mandated that there should be a primary school within 1 kilometre of every household), then the KGBV was often the best option.

Now in her early twenties, Vibha was a petite young woman, dressed in a soft cream-and-red-coloured saree, a warm jacket and a gold-trimmed translucent dupatta that had fallen from her head and was draped over her shoulder. Vibha explained with relish the opportunity she had had at the KGBV to visit Mount Abu on a school trip. As we continued to chat, she drew breath, about to go on, when Dinesh jumped in: 'The world today is built for the educated!' he declared dramatically.

A profound statement from the proud and eloquent man who sat opposite me on a black moulded, plastic chair in his immaculate courtyard. To our left, through the boundary wall gate, the comings and goings of the village were visible. To our right was Dinesh's simple but attractive two-room whitewashed bungalow, a brick-built pukka[12] home to a family of seven children. The family had now shrunk with the passing of time, as the children stepped out into the world with families, lives of their own and with their education.

'And,' Dinesh paused dramatically. 'I only know this because *I* am educated,' he continued, with a proud emphasis on the 'I'. 'The uneducated will have no place in this world, and if you are *not* educated, you will be exploited like animals.'

Just as he said this a herd of goats passed by the courtyard gate, their discordant bells jangling, and Dinesh nodded in their direction with a knowing look. His allusion was not lost on me. He is retired now and has a small strip of land that he farms just behind the house. He also looks after the vacant properties of the families from the village, who have migrated to Udaipur or Mumbai. Families who needed someone to keep an eye on their native home while they live and work full-time in the city. Everyone in the village trusts Dinesh Ji, as a respected member of various village committees. But he was once a skilled stonemason, working on the Akshardham Temple in Gujarat. A skilled stone mason, with a tenth-pass education.

'I'm strong!' he announced, flexing muscles that we of course couldn't see beneath his lilac kurta, but you could tell from his hands that he was indeed strong and had certainly worked hard. He loved to work with his hands, he told us, but, as he reiterated, he was *educated*.

Today, fifteen years after we first met her, it took us a while to get to speak to Vibha herself, as her energetic father held court. It was evident that a hierarchy still existed in the family. Shrouded in a red dupatta, Mamta, Vibha's mother, joined us. We all beamed and greeted her, but we could only assume she was smiling too. It wasn't until later when we persuaded her to lift her veil that we saw her gleaming eyes and contented face. She moved to crouch at her husband's feet, until we all leapt to *our* feet and insisted she sit with us on a chair.

I felt for her as she sat uncomfortably, not used to the furniture. My mind wandered, and I thought about her life. When we eventually saw her smile, Mamta looked older than me, but we were likely the same age. A harsh environment and difficult life had meted out more on her face than mine. She had adult children; mine were still in their teens. I couldn't help thinking that I might have been born here. This could have been me.

Dinesh's animal analogy sat somewhat uncomfortably with me, particularly as it was clear that his own wife was not an educated woman. But what he was really trying to explain was the need for education so that everyone could understand their basic human rights, rights that an animal does not have.

'Everyone should read the Constitution!' he declared, waving his fist in the air like a revolutionary. He went on to explain to us how we all needed to know our rights because with knowledge of our rights we would be able to hold politicians to account, know how to vote and make informed choices. 'If we don't have education, we don't know our rights and we will be exploited like sheep or goats!' And there he was again, back to the animals. This was not the conversation I had anticipated having as we visited Vibha, but it was and is a conversation that so clearly supports the unarguable premise that education is every girl's right.

Dinesh has a point. The world is made for the educated, and as Nagina Bano showed us all those years ago, 'a little bit of education' can be a matter of survival. It can be the difference between holding on to your assets and being defrauded. It can be the window to the world so that you can stand up for yourself and avoid exploitation.

It is perhaps more pronounced in pockets of India, but across the world as well we see communities living in multiple centuries in parallel. Without an education a person is trapped in a bygone era, unable to access and benefit from the progress the twenty-first century has seen in terms of communication, transport, healthcare, political engagement, etc. Nations too are held back when a majority of their citizens are unable to read or write. A quality education can change the life of an individual and family in just one generation. Education means that you can advocate for yourself and have the agency to make the choices you want for yourself in the world.

Nagina's and Dinesh's words remind me of what Nelson Mandela said: 'Education is the most powerful weapon which you can use to change the world.'[13]

Despite this, globally, 133 million girls still remain out of school.[14]

2

On the Margins

'Go to the people on the margins … If you live near the crossroads or if you live near a river, you're going to be okay. But if you live on the margins … the world is going to forget about you.'

—Hans Rosling to Melinda Gates[1]

There is no doubt in my mind that the lack of a quality education is a barrier to the dignity of a girl living in today's world. Being denied an education is the deepest form of inequality, rendering a girl powerless and dependent. Behind every illiterate woman is a girl who was not allowed to go to school. But what I wanted to understand when I began exploring this subject was why girls were still not going to school in certain areas. What were the barriers? Who were the out-of-school girls and why were they being denied this basic right? It was 2007, and I started by going deeper into rural Pali with some of our first team members and asking a lot of questions.

Physical Margins

India is a country of twenty-eight states and eight union territories, including over 6,60,000 villages that are home to roughly 65 per cent of its population.[2] All villages are not identical and their locations and access to them can vary dramatically. Some are close to towns and cities, where progress is much more visible; some are close to the crossroads, where public transport connects them to the wider world; while some are remote and inaccessible, especially if on the wrong side of the river or a hill. Physical distance to school can be the first barrier to a girl's education.

'The school is far' was a constant refrain from all the girls and parents we met.

I was in Sumerpur block[3] where I had come to meet Ramchandra, one of our team members. The plan was to talk to girls there who were not enrolled in school. Trailing Ramchandra that day was quite an undertaking. I might have been forgiven for thinking we were on a hike, off the beaten path, meandering through hills, exploring new terrain. But Ramchandra knew exactly where he was going, none of this was new to him. He was on a mission, but he also had a laidback air about him and a confidence that belied a great sense of being part of the land, native to this very place, very much at home.

Once we reached the top of the hill, Ramchandra extended his arm in the direction of the sun. It took a minute or two for my eyes to adjust to the late morning glare, which bleached the sky as I tried to make out what he was showing me. The landscape was a series of undulating hills and valleys, some with 45 degree inclines we were about to scale. Some hills had animal sheds, some had homes. They were indistinguishable to me. But Ramchandra knew everyone, all 400 families. He knew who lived where and who we needed to visit. But as far as the eye could see, there was no obvious village.

This village is indeed a collection of seven hamlets with very little that brings them together as a village—there is certainly no village hub. It lies 60 kilometres from Pali city, a three-hour walk to the nearest medical facility to the south and a three-hour walk to the nearest bank to the north. A towering mobile phone mast sits bang in the middle of the arid landscape like an elongated Eiffel Tower. There are five to six hours of electricity on most days and the fields are criss-crossed by precarious-looking electricity wires—wires that carry the charge for the phones of the village men but don't carry much for the girls. There is no running water, cooking is done with firewood (gathered and carried by the girls), water is hauled up from open wells (always collected by the girls), and there is one road that winds its way through the clusters of homes, a kutcha[4] road. No asphalt or cement. We were truly on the margins.

It seemed a dry, barren location, underpopulated and remote. But on closer inspection, it was possible to make out individual fields—a patchwork of yellow and green discrete crops, grasses that would provide feed for livestock and wheat for bread. Much of it was parched and brown, but where the soil was good enough and irrigation possible, every part of the land had purpose. Fruit trees had sticks leaning up against them revealing that they were regularly harvested. There was no windfall on the ground, every fruit was put to use. As I took shelter from the scorching heat for a few moments under one such tree, Ramchandra picked up the stick and shook the tree vigorously, catching the Indian plums as they toppled and handing me a few to try. They were tart.

The primary and secondary schools were near the main road, just after the crossroad as you turned left towards the village before the road turned kutcha. But neither school was really *in* the village, and not really near where most people lived. Earlier in the day we had driven past the schools and left the buildings behind, reaching the end of the road in perhaps ten or fifteen minutes, but that was by car. No one in this village drove or owned a car. Once the road ended, we set off on foot along paths you would be forgiven for missing. Paths that didn't exist. Working backwards, school was perhaps a good hour and a half on foot from the houses we were about to visit, and I thought to myself: 'Twice a day, in the heat of the sun, that is *far*.' In our hardy trainers and adult legs, we walked and walked, we climbed, we paused to catch our breath—and in three hours we covered four homes.

I felt a similar sense of living on the margins when visiting villages near the Bandi River. One such village had more going for it than some—it was a little closer to the nearest town, but it had a river running through it. A river that shrunk in the dry months and was easy enough to cross when the boatman was there, or the farmer with his raft and paddle.

It meandered rather than flowed. On occasion, it dried out to the extent that there were stepping stones. But for three months of the year, this river filled and flowed. There was no bridge, and there were days, many days, when the boatman didn't go, and the farmer's raft wasn't strong enough. In the monsoon, the Bandi River was a torrent; it was angry and defiant and had no empathy for the families who lived on the 'wrong' side. On the 'wrong' side, you didn't or couldn't go to school; this was another village on the margins.

There is no denying it was also a challenge for the boys to go to school in these villages. But parents were less worried about the journey when it came to their sons. If it was far, they could cope. The monsoon waters were sometimes insurmountable for boys *and* girls. But the distance was worse for girls, it really was. They would likely have walked the same distance already before school to fetch water, and the road might involve walking past the liquor store or a gathering of village men. Most girls in these remote villages did not go to school.

Economic Margins

Vibha lived closer to the centre of her village—distance was less of a barrier for her—but Dinesh, despite his education, struggled when it came to his income.

'I remember in the monsoon waking up in a pool of water, as the roof always leaked!' Vibha reflected when we continued our conversation with her.

She giggled, but it was clear that this was not a humorous memory; the laugh was more to mask the image she had just dug up of very difficult times. I noticed how she glanced over to the roof of her rebuilt home, her secure roof. I could almost feel her relief. Kutcha homes are built from natural materials, much like kutcha roads. They are constructed using mud and then bamboo, stone, thatch or unburnt brick. Shelter, of course, but no real protection from the elements.

Roti, kapda aur makaan (food, clothing and shelter) are the basic needs, but all too often, on the margins, these needs fail to be met. Life for Dinesh, Vibha's father, must have been a struggle, in spite of his education and his good job as a mason. And for Mamta to feed so many mouths, must have been nigh on impossible. They would have been eligible for monthly rations from the government: a bag of wheat, rice, daal, salt, oil, sugar, tea and a few extra spices to supplement what they were growing in the field behind the house. But as her family grew, for a while, Mamta's culinary repertoire shrunk to an all-time low. The year Aarti, Vibha's youngest sibling, was born, Mamta had nine mouths to feed. This was when three meals a day reduced to one, and one meal became dry roti.

Vibha's older sister would often go to work with Dinesh and help out at the building site, earning a little more to help Mamta put food on the table. But finances were always a struggle. 'I remember times when we didn't eat vegetables for weeks,' she told us. 'Things were very difficult.'

They even had to share clothes. Vibha recalled this with that same nervous laugh. 'Two pairs of chuddies for seven children! We were a large family, which didn't help our financial condition. And then there were the loans. We were always having to pay back loans.' They never took a loan from the bank, Vibha explained. It was always from someone in the village, and the interest payments took a further toll on the monthly finances. One of her younger sisters had very poor health and Dinesh had to constantly borrow money here and there for her medical treatment.

This is what economic marginalization really means. Poverty contributes in a big way to girls being out of school. It leads parents to prioritize a boy's education over a girl's. There is a belief that boys will work, contribute to household income and look after parents in their old age; hence, they get to go to school. Sons are educated to earn. Daughters are not. The consequence of poverty is a girl missing school or a girl required to work out of the home—like Vibha's sisters who helped Dinesh on the construction site—or a girl required to work inside the home, helping with household work to enable both parents to go and earn.

Living on the margins all too often means living in poverty, and in India today we still have an estimated 370 million people living in this level of poverty. That is roughly a quarter of our population. When you are home to one-sixth of humanity, when indeed you are the largest nation in the world (when we sneaked past China), that is a sizable chunk of the entire world's people who exist below the poverty line. Five out of every six of the world's poor live in sub-Saharan Africa or South Asia, and despite a rapid decline in these figures in India, it is still the single country that is home to the majority, at approximately 21 per cent.[5]

But what is economic marginalization? What does it mean to be poor? When I think back to some of the darkest days of my childhood in Delhi, I knew what it meant to me. The shame of telling my classmates at school that I only ever ate khichdi when we were supposed to be having a discussion about our families' cultural heritage and our favourite dishes. My classmates talked about biryani and butter chicken, idli, sambar, puris, aamras and paneer. But we ate khichdi. Every day. With an occasional squeeze of lemon or teaspoon of Dalda vanaspati. My mother cooked on a small electric coil cooking heater, and when there was no electricity, which was often, she would battle with the kerosene pressure stove which had an intricate and complex choreography to be lit. It was a time-consuming and very frustrating process. I lived in eternal fear of the kerosene pump stove exploding and never went near it.

There are of course the official definitions of poverty. When the government agent knocks on your door and paints the BPL (Below Poverty Line) number on your wall, this means that each member of the household has a daily income per day of less than 150 rupees and spends less than 27 rupees.[6] But poverty data is severely lacking since the 2021 census was not carried out, and revisions to this have still not been made, in the light of potential advances over the past fourteen years. The poverty I experienced cannot begin to be compared to this, I admit. But still I felt it, I still felt poor, and when we first met Vibha, back in 2008, she felt poor too.

Poverty forces families to work and make choices. And these choices involve deciding who goes to work, who stays at home and allows both parents to work, and who goes to school. Poverty sometimes means that no children in a family get to go to school. But invariably, if there is a choice, it is the boys who go. Girls stay at home and work.

Social Margins

The Indian caste system is an added, unpalatable but persistent determinant in this lottery of life. If you live near the crossroads, you are likely to belong to a higher caste, and essentially to have more privilege. This means you live close to public services and have access to government schemes. If you belong to a lower caste, you likely live up and over the hill or across the river. And the further you get away from the main road, from the school or the temple, the further you are from the 'right' side of the river, the deeper you fall into the social margins, not just the physical. This is not about whether you are a stone mason, whether you work on the MGNREGA scheme or whether you work at all. This is also fundamentally about *who* you are.

Five of every six people in India living in multidimensional poverty live in a Scheduled Tribe (ST)-, Scheduled Caste (SC)- or Other Backward Caste (OBC)-headed household.[7] From the very beginning of our work in Pali we knew that we needed to ask the right questions and gather the right data—and even at this early stage we were seeing patterns—95 per cent of the out-of-school girls we found in 2007 were from families categorized as OBC, ST or SC. The equalization of opportunity through education has not yet been fully realized for any of these communities. And it is not just caste—your religion can also mean you are on the social margins. Muslims in India, for example, are often described as a hidden underclass; they have the lowest asset and consumption levels among all the religions.[8]

A community particularly vulnerable to exclusion is the Gadulia Lohar community living along the train tracks in

Falna. A nomadic community, they were originally Rajput iron smiths, and in Rajasthan are today categorized as MBC, members of the *Most* Backward Classes. They struggled, living in tented dwellings often made partly from their bullock carts (gadulia, meaning cart). They led such a different life in their temporary homes that sadly became far from temporary—this particular group in Falna had failed to move from beside the rail tracks for years. Sheltering beneath canvas, they oftentimes missed out on schemes, missed out on being counted and missed out on any welfare—including rations and work.

'School isn't a place for people like us!' was a statement we got used to hearing.

The social dynamics of a village were always very clear. Who lives where, which community lives where, who can use the water pump when: This was all common knowledge. In cities, too, housing societies had categories. I lived a large part of my childhood in DDA (Delhi Development Authority) colonies. The homes the government built were demarcated clearly along its hierarchy. You had HIG flats for the 'High-Income Group', MIG flats for the 'Middle-Income Group and LIG flats for the 'Low-Income Group'. Below these clearly demarcated homes were the most 'backward' class of government housing: the one-room 'janta flats'. These were small single rooms with a bathroom and toilet. Families either cooked in the room itself, or, like my mother, in the narrow corridor that connected the room to the toilet and bathroom. It was in the Janta flats that I spent part of my growing up and so was well aware of my status and position in the world. Even as a child, just as I did, people 'knew their place', and that place was both physical and social.

Names that Reveal a Mindset

Distance to school, poverty and caste affect both boys and girls. And yes, boys are also out of school. But why is it that only 49 per cent of countries have reached gender parity in primary education? At the lower and upper secondary levels, the gap is even wider, with only 42 per cent and a staggering 24 per cent of countries respectively having achieved gender parity in their education systems.[9] And why? Well, this is essentially because below class, caste and in other contexts, race, comes gender. Being a woman and a girl amplifies the negative impacts of all the other contributing factors. These names embody the way gender multiplies disadvantage: they mark girls as lesser, undeserving and expendable. It is the intimate, everyday violence of being named as though your life does not matter. Here are some of them:

Aachuki: Arrived
Nakushi: Unwanted
Faaltu: Useless
Manbhaari: Heavy Heart
Maafi: Sorry
Dhaapu: Fed up
Naraaz: Angry
Galla: Stop
Antimbala: Last One

I don't usually review our out-of-school girl lists in such great detail. Over the years, they have become digitized, and I see the dashboard, the summary data, the numbers. The field teams see the faces. It is they who hear the names. But curiosity got the better of me. I had recently met a little girl called Maafi, meaning 'sorry'. Daughter of Hemlal and Lalita. A little girl, and yet her parents' apology, so when I got back to the Mumbai office, I asked the data team to run some lists for me.

After a while the words and letters just started to swim in front of my eyes as I couldn't quite believe what I was reading. The spreadsheet started off as I read from left to right: State: Rajasthan, District: Banswara, Block: Ghatol, Village ... then a code, a survey date, parents' names. Everything seemed normal. And then, the same girls' names, over and over and over again. As I read, my eyes moved from village to village, household number to household number, but the girls' names remained the same: Maafi. Line after line. Maafi. Maafi. Maafi. Sorry. Sorry. Sorry. I just kept on scrolling, clenching the computer mouse in my hand, until the spreadsheet went empty again. I let out a sigh, and the repetition stopped, but my eyes welled up, my vision of the spreadsheet got distorted and the tears began.

'How many girls have we found with that name?' I asked our impact manager, Akhil. 'How many Maafis are there?' I hesitated to ask as I wasn't sure I really wanted to know.

'Four hundred and five,' Akhil responded. His tone was flat, like he was himself apologizing for that number. According to these lists, we found:

405 girls called Maafi, which means 'sorry'.
566 girls called Naaraz, which means 'angry'.
1,516 girls—a staggering 1,516—called Dhaapu, meaning 'fed up'.
And 233 girls called Antimbala, which means the 'last girl'.

In India, we think deeply about our names. The naming convention includes a given name and then a secondary name that might be a surname or patronym, perhaps a reference to a child's native village, a parent's occupation or caste. Given names are decided upon with a lot of thought; they all have meanings. And that is why the above list leaves me cold. What must the prevailing emotion be when you call your girl 'useless' or 'unwanted'? When I think about every one of those girls, every one of those parents, weighed down by anger, frustration and disappointment at having a girl, my resolve is hardened. My mission is set.

And these names reveal a mindset. From the day these little girls enter the world, they are considered a burden. They are held back by a mindset that keeps them out of school, denies them an education and sets them on a narrow pathway that leads to marriage and motherhood, almost completely missing out on anything that could remotely be described as a childhood. And their names reflect this story. A girl Arrives. Unwanted. Her parents see her as Useless. They have a Heavy Heart, they are Sorry, Fed up, even Angry. They make a plea: Stop! Enough! And they hope she is the Last Girl.

I came to this realization when we were ramping up our data systems. A spreadsheet had never before shocked me quite so much. But this one did, and from then on, I became more and more intrigued by the link between a name and a mindset. Every time I went into the field I wanted to know more about the girls and their parents' choice of names. Sometimes, the more you are aware of something, the more you see it, even if you aren't looking, and this is exactly what happened. Stories just kept appearing for me, in the newspaper, online, through well-respected media houses, like Zubair Ahmed's BBC story[10] that I found. As per the story, 285 girls were found in the district of Satara in Maharashtra who had all been called Nakusha, which means 'unwanted'. The story had a positive ending, in a way, as Zubair was reporting on a government-led ceremony to rename all the girls. They had now been allowed to choose new names, like Kiran, meaning 'ray of light', or Ashmita, meaning 'very tough'. But in this relatively sparsely populated district that is home to the popular hill station of Mahabaleshwar as well as a handful of spectacular forts, it shocked me that so many girls, from babies right up to twenty-year-old women, were carrying this bleak, hurtful name. Unwanted.

The names became stranger the more I read. One girl I read about in the newspaper more recently had been named 'Missed Call'—as her father, Bharat, said: 'Antima is my second daughter as we wished her to be the last daughter. But then we had a third daughter. We named her "Missed Call", because we missed out on a boy.' Their fourth child was a boy, but just think about what those girls must feel to have such negative names, and their brother celebrated so much more.

A mechanic I learnt about in the north-east of India called his sons Firstgear and Secondgear, and his daughter Reverse. These girls' names kept going round and round in my head and I couldn't stop thinking what it must really feel like when you are driven to choose such a name. And then if the girls themselves feel sad or embarrassed, I wondered.

'No. There are many girls in my school with such names. It's normal,' one girl interviewed for an article explained. Her name was Guarantee (as in, please God, *guarantee* us a boy next).

Having had conversations with so many families over the years, it dawned on me how hard it must be to escape the mindset that a goat is an asset and a girl is a liability. We are back to Dinesh's animal analogy again. In many village communities, families articulate their wealth through the number of goats they own—in the village your wealth is made visible through the size of your herd; that's how you garner respect. Goats are the prized asset, sometimes even a source of envy. The opposite is true for girls. Girls are not an asset. Girls are a liability, a source of pity across the village.

Being Born at All

A preference for sons is widespread in India even today. In the early 2000s the story of India's missing girls was widely told. UNFPA, the UN's Population Fund, calculated an average of 5,80,000 missing female births each year in the six years up to 2007 when India's sex ratio at birth was at its lowest.[11] As recently as 2020 the agency estimated that India accounted for one-third of the world's such girls, and by 'missing girls', we mean quite literally girls who should have been born but weren't. The invention of amniocentesis hastened the ability of families to make this choice, the choice not to have a girl. The outlawing of sex-selective abortions in 1994 attempted to halt it. But the law can only go so far when 'girl aversion' is so strong.

Andu knew this aversion only too well. We met her when we started work in her village in around 2010. Andu was an outlier in the community, an outlier in much of our programme, to be honest—aged twenty-five, she had finally passed her twelfth-grade exams. Andu was educated. When she married at twenty-three, she requested to continue her education, but her husband and in-laws refused to give her permission. And, yes, permission had to be sought. This was distressing for Andu, an ambitious, independent young woman who had dreams of a marriage and children, no doubt, but also planned for independence and knowledge. When she did give birth, the distress was amplified beyond cognition to a new mother. Her in-laws wanted a boy. Andu gave birth to a girl. She was told she had to kill her baby, and if she wouldn't do it, they would. 'Take the embers from the fire,' they told her. 'Let her drink ash and then she will die.'

'*Woh usko ek bojh samajhte.* They told me she was a burden, a liability,' Andu explained in a voice that revealed an incredulity, even that day when we first met her. At that time everything was undoubtedly still very raw, and her daughter was a thriving two-year-old toddler. Today, Andu's daughter is studying in eleventh grade, and she still carries the emotional scars.

The only thing Andu could do was flee. She picked up her three-day-old baby and ran. But where to?

To get to her parents she had to navigate a dense forest. And if she came out the other side, she didn't even know if her family would allow her home. There would be shame, there would be anger. But she had no choice. Having given birth seventy-two hours earlier, in pain, exhaustion and terror, she began the 20 kilometre escape to her parents' home. I had absolutely no concept of what this must have felt like. After both the births of my two daughters, I was holed up at home for two weeks, surrounded by help and surrounded by joy. Yes, I put up with the odd comment from a distant aunty when my second was born and there was, in my wider family circle, still that hope and expectation of a boy. But the idea of running 20 kilometres straight after childbirth is beyond comprehension.

Being Born a Girl

The Indian government, over ten years ago, recognized this as a problem, a serious problem, and in 2014 Beti Bachao, Beti Padhao (Save the Girl, Educate the Girl) was launched as a high-profile nationwide scheme in response to the falling proportion of female births, still worryingly low at the 2011 census. By calling for the nation to 'save the girl', the scheme acknowledged the female existential threat, a threat to girls both born and unborn. But when we first started our work, this was not the case.

'In our village we celebrate the birth of a boy. The house becomes like the scene of a festival. The beating of the copper thali [platter] chimes across the village. Some families even fire a gun!' Vibha announced this with a serious intensity, trying to shock us a little. 'We all love the birth of a boy, as sometimes we even get laddoos!' she continued.

Her eyes warmed and sparkled, and I could certainly relate to her excitement at the thought of a laddoo. I too had always loved the sugary taste of one. After the birth of a boy, the first Holi is celebrated like a wedding. The joy Vibha's neighbours had felt at the birth of their sons was palpable. Even in Vibha's eyes as she told us the story of her village, I could understand that feeling. But then her eyes dropped. 'When a girl is born, there is nothing like that. Nothing like that happens for a girl. There is no celebration.'

The birth of a girl was met with silence. Vibha too had left us in silence.

You might be born far from the main road. You might be born into a Scheduled Tribe family. You might be born where government policies don't reach. But if you are born a girl as well, you will not only have practical and geographical hurdles to overcome, you will also have to fight against mindset, against the idea that you are a liability, that a goat is worth more than you. And you will have to fight for your education, your health, your well-being and any semblance of equality with your brother.

Time and time again we were meeting families where there were older girls who were either never enrolled in school or had dropped out after a few years, and yet their brothers set off every morning to the local school. And what were all these girls doing if they weren't in school?

A Girl's Work

As we pulled out of the village with Ramchandra, after our visit to four girls on the hill, Poonam, one of the girls, was halfway down the valley behind her house with her ox, scything grass to feed her and to feed the goats at home. We had only left Varju twenty minutes ago, but already she too could be seen at the water pit hauling up a bucket with a colourful patchwork of dirty clothes at her feet. It was time for the laundry. She waved across the field with a smile, and I wondered if she was sorry or relieved that we had left. And just as we approached our car, three girls we hadn't yet met wandered past us, barefoot. Their bodies were like the slimmest of sapling trees beneath a pile of branches balanced on their heads, wider than they were tall. The firewood had arrived. We thought we had made good progress when chatting with some of these parents, but no sooner had we left that the girls' work began again.

My daughters were with me during one of those visits and that image of the girls and the firewood has never really left us. The procession was like a set of Russian dolls. The lady at the front with the biggest bundle was perhaps the grandmother of the group. Behind her the girls and their bundles shrunk incrementally until the very last girl, who still carried a substantial pile but was practically naked, with just a tiny little cloth around her waist—she could not have been more than about four years old. The words of my daughters still haunt my dreams: 'Mummy, why isn't Educate Girls helping those girls?' And at that time, I had no answer.

Women spend 2.5 times more hours each day on unpaid care work than men. Girls learn this early and, globally, contribute 160 million more hours daily to unpaid care and domestic work than boys.[12] And that's a global figure. I can't help thinking that in these villages the percentage is considerably higher. Work is an interesting barometer when understanding patriarchy. There is an expectation that girls need to contribute. In Vibha's family, it was her sister who helped her father with his masonry work when finances were tight, while her brother went to school.

'We girls were the first to get up, and the last to go to bed,' she nonchalantly stated, affirming the mindset in this simple observation. Girls will do all the housework. Girls will look after the animals. Girls will collect the water and the wood. Girls will earn if needed. Girls will take on anything that is required of them. Sleep and education will always take a back seat. This is the mindset.

Education is an investment. There is a cost, even when education is ostensibly free. Uniform, school bags, transport to school. And then, more importantly, the *opportunity* cost. Families on the margins need their daughters to work—invariably domestic work at home—to enable both parents to earn. Sometimes it's agricultural work, tending to the crops or livestock. And sometimes it's working to earn, making incense sticks, working for a large-scale farmer on his harvest. Child labour is still prevalent, and families will choose their daughter first so their son can still go to school.

'Why invest in someone who soon enough will be of value to another family, not our own?' 'Girls will leave!' One parent described it to me like this: Investing in their daughters was like 'watering the neighbour's plants'.

The Size of the Liability

But what is the size of this 'liability'? Where does this idea of a burden come from? One of the biggest costs around which household economics in India revolves is marriage. Marriages are costly, and it costs the family of the bride, not the groom. Despite the practice of dowry being illegal since 1961, it very much lives on today and is something that features in the balance sheet of life as soon as a girl is born. The size of the wedding and the dowry can determine a good husband, a suitable boy. The wedding and the dowry can, in turn, determine the size of the loan and the extent of the debt, and therein lies the liability. After the wedding, the girl moves to the husband's home and although there is one less mouth to feed, there are also fewer hands to work, and a family's daughter becomes another family's daughter-in-law. Having a girl is expensive. Having a boy is not.

'What use is she to us? The boys need the *good* food!' Vibha was mimicking one of her neighbours when she made this emphatic statement. She asserted the village opinion with a tone of resignation—it's the boys who need the investment, the good food, good health and, of course, education. And this mindset, this apathy towards girls, manifests in a widespread neglect of girls' health and well-being.[13]

'In our village the boys are given ghee laddoos in winter. But not the girls.' She had lost count of the times she had watched the boys lick their fingers and could only imagine the taste herself. 'After they cook and serve everyone, the girls eat last and eat the least,' Vibha explained.

We feed the boys, and we feed the goats. We invest in our assets, but not in our liabilities.

Another one of our students was Swati, a deeply focused learner. But she was tired. It was clear at every session she spent with us at Educate Girls that she had been up before dawn and had done the equivalent of a full day's work before arriving at the camp to study, dusty and weary. Swati lived a day within a day. She had dropped out of school when she was eleven years old as her father had fallen ill. We had found twenty-one girls in her village in a similar situation. Along with the cooking, cleaning, fetching of water and doing other household chores, it was Swati's job now to look after the cows and the goats, and they were of critical importance to the family. Seven goats was a respectable number. Her father was a man respected for his goats. So when Swati asked to travel to a town two hours away to take her tenth-grade exams, he refused on the day of the exam, saying: 'Who will take care of the goats?' His tone assumed this was the obvious question and the obvious answer was that she, Swati, would of course not take the exam.

Because it was on the day of the exam, we had no time to find solutions or try negotiating with him. Swati ran to her Educate Girls team member, Pallavi. Pallavi was adamant that Swati would get to take her exams. She was not going to let five months of study go to waste. She was not going to let a goat get in the way of her studious pupil's opportunity, her potential lifeline. So Pallavi hurried to Swati's house.

'I'll take care of the goats while she goes for the exam!' Pallavi swapped her students for seven goats.

Pallavi spent the afternoon walking the hillside on the edge of Swati's village. The goats grazed. And Swati took the bus to the town with nine other girls from her village. She sat her exam and she wrote her papers. And the goats ate, the goats drank. Swati's father remained indifferent, but Swati took her tenth-grade exams and she passed.

The Meaning of the Margins

When physical, economic and social margins align against you during a crisis, you are hit the hardest, whether that is a climate crisis or a health crisis like the pandemic. You are the hardest hit in natural disasters, in wars and conflicts. And you will be affected the most by the climate crisis. If you are on the margins, you are more dependent upon the land for your income and sustenance, so you are more susceptible to what the climate metes out on you and your crops. In the rains, the floods and heatwaves that are all becoming worse and more frequent, resilience is low on the margins and costs are high. What might have been sick leave for one person is complete exclusion from the world of work for others as livelihoods are disrupted or destroyed. A daily wage is just that. If you can't work, you won't get paid. If you don't get paid, you won't eat. And with the floods come the insects and disease, and medical costs can throw a family into crippling debt.

The first time I saw a Universal Thermal Climate Index map of India and that practically the whole country was coloured blood red, *my* blood began to boil.[14] On 30 April 2023, hundreds died as a result of the soaring temperatures and resulting 'heat stress'—a term that sounds like we are all making a 'bit of a fuss', but when you dig into the science of it, heat stress is devastating and lethal. As the temperature approaches the body temperature of 37 degrees Celsius the body is not able to cool itself by sweating; even at 31 degrees Celsius dangerously little sweat can evaporate. Sustained exposure to 35 degrees Celsius is considered fatal.

As I sat with Vibha again the following year, a small glass of chai in one hand and a damp hanky in the other, dabbing the ticklish beads of sweat that constantly rolled down my temples, it was difficult to imagine what that April heat might have felt like. I was grateful that moisture was still trickling, even when it went down the edge of my nose and into my mouth with an inelegant salty prick on the tongue. I was in the shade. Vibha had been going out to work in April. Now a community nurse, Vibha's job was to travel from village to village, house to house, meeting women and following up after the birth of their children. She at least got to sit in the shade in one home after another, but travelling around each day is exhausting and, on more than one occasion, she told me that she had collapsed. She was a proud young lady, not keen to show vulnerability. But it was clear that what the environment was meting out was taking a toll. And just think of the women working under the MNREGA scheme, outside labouring all day long.

Your vulnerability is the highest when you are an out-of-school girl because you exist on the deepest margins of caste, class and gender. You have the least tools to help you build resilience, your mobility is restricted, opportunities to get ahead grow non-existent, making you ripe for exploitation.

A story I had heard many times from girls belonging to socially marginalized communities: If their mother was sick, they immediately stepped into a caregiving role at far too young an age. Young girls took the place of the mother—either going out to work or working at home as the primary caretaker. Rekha was one such girl. An ambitious young woman who despite lacking role models in her community—the Bhil tribe[15]—had managed to stay in school up to grade eleven. She had three brothers, two older than her and one younger. They all enjoyed going to school together. But when their mother unexpectedly fell ill as her eleventh-grade exams loomed, there was no question that Rekha would stay at home, take on the household chores and care for their mother. Her brothers were not giving exams that year. But it was Rekha who had to stay at home. At first she tried to keep up with her studies, but eventually she had to drop out. Her head mistress suggested that given her absence she might not clear the board exam, and the school didn't want their ranking to be negatively affected. Eleven grades fought for and nearly completed, and then Rekha was forced to abandon her education.

If you live on the edge of the village or the wrong side of the river, not only will a normal monsoon increase the likelihood of disease and fever but the rains are more likely to prevent children from getting to school, and home and schools will be more likely to be damaged in a flash flood. And there isn't really anything like a 'normal' monsoon anymore. Extreme weather events have increased by 80 per cent in the last two decades and are getting more extreme—24.1 million children in India are affected annually by floods, cyclones, heatwaves and other similar emergencies, and now 80 per cent of the population in India resides in districts exposed to extreme hazardous conditions.[16]

Even if a girl doesn't drop out in these cases, interruptions start to fully disrupt her education, and that of the boys too. There is increased absenteeism in getting to school or being in school becomes harder, if you have to navigate a flood or extreme heat. These all result in missing days here and there and even days at a stretch. Extreme heat has an impact on cognitive development after prolonged exposure, and more immediately on concentration. Absenteeism leads to learning lags and learning lags lead to either poor learning outcomes or dropping out. The fact that you are on the margins affects you even if you have managed to make it to school. The weather is out of your control.

When I arrived in Durga's village, I was already feeling the heat. It was late May and the monsoon rains were nowhere in sight. The heavy clouds had yet to gather. My conversation with Durga started much like any other:

'Water has to be collected before dawn as the well is so far. It takes me over an hour to reach, queue and then when I get home I have to finish all my other chores.' This is what she told me when I met her a year after we had helped enrol her in school. 'But on Fridays, I don't go,' she told me point blank.

My enquiry as to why led to the explanation that Friday was bath day.

'So you are not allowed to go to school on the day you have a bath?' I asked, puzzled.

'No.' She elaborated. 'On bath days, I have to collect the water twice. It takes me around four hours altogether to go and come twice, so I don't have time for school.' Bath day is, of course, essential. Since the well dried up, it was already problematic and she had been reduced to bathing only once a week. Durga looked quite forlorn when she explained how much she had been bullied at school for not bathing and wearing dirty clothes.

But the weather spares no one, surely. Well, that is not the case. Women and girls are far more likely to die in climate-related disasters than men—some say as many as fourteen times more likely. Gender disaster vulnerability is linked to knowledge, decision-making and access to resources, and when 2,50,000 people died in the 2004 tsunami, some reports concluded that around 70 per cent of the dead were women. In the Bangladesh cyclone in 1991, 90 per cent of those who died were female.[17]

I wasn't surprised when I read that girls in crisis settings are two and a half times more likely to be out of primary school and 90 per cent more likely to be out of secondary school than boys when living through war, insurgency or a natural disaster.[18] But what we have to realize is that none of this is biological, but social—this is not because of our make, this is just because we were born female. We were born as girls. We are lucky to live in relative stability in India, but crises hit nonetheless, and the knowledge that girls will bear the brunt is something that keeps me awake at night and drives my mission to get girls into school.

As I started to dig deeper into the problem of marginalization, one thing became more and more clear. Of course, marginalization affects boys too, and life is more difficult all genders when you live far from school, in poverty and you belong to a Scheduled Tribe, Scheduled Caste or other minority group. But on top of all these factors, being born across the river, being born poor, being born into a tribal family—if you are on the margins and born *a girl* everything is amplified.

The world today is still built by and for men, and as a girl, the mountain you have to climb is the highest, because you have to overcome something invisible: a mindset. Government schemes like work programmes, employment guarantees, rations, help to build permanent housing—all these are important support and all these incentives can help. Reservations are in place to try and overcome the discrimination of the caste system. But as a woman or a girl, fighting a mindset is perhaps the most complicated problem of all.

When you are a girl at the intersection of physical, economic and social marginalization, and the prevailing mindset in your village is that you are a liability, then your right to an education becomes a distant dream. And not just in India, but around the world where this intersection happens, marriage and motherhood is the only path. Where poverty meets patriarchy, where goats are prized and girls are not, and where the climate crisis hits hardest: there you will find a concentration of out-of-school girls, indeed today you will still find 133 million.

PART II

Finding Antimbala

3

Changing a School of Thought

'It takes a village to educate a child.'

—Traditional proverb

Picture a girl who has been excluded from school. She is dressed in a faded salwar-kameez. Her feet are bare. She is crouched in the corner of a dark room. She rarely speaks, but when she does, her voice is deep and husky from years of cooking over an open fire; she is skinny from malnutrition, and she is tired from anaemia. She struggles to make eye contact. She has no self-esteem. She has been hollowed out by patriarchy and a feeling of being worthless. This is a problem that I know still exists in our world, despite economic growth and innovation, despite everything we all call 'progress'. This is the problem we all need to see.

Now imagine the same little girl dressed in a clean, pressed uniform. She wears her hair in two neat plaits tied with red ribbons. She has a school bag strapped to her back and is walking confidently down the road towards school. She is smiling, chatting with her friends. She has a hot lunch in school, learns in the classroom and plays with her fellow students. Now she holds her head high.

We knew out-of-school girls were most likely to be on the margins. So we had to work on the margins: geographically, this meant working in the most rural, remote and tribal areas. Economic margins meant working with the poorest of the poor. Social margins meant most of those we worked with were not only rural but also from tribal, lower-caste or minority communities. But once at the margins, the problem was mindset.

The very idea that a girl's worth is lesser than a boy is a mindset, a school of thought. A way of thinking that can stand in the way of a girl accessing her fundamental human rights. If the problem is mindset, then the solution has to be human! I had to learn to change mindsets. But how? As we know from living in a highly polarized world, that is easier said than done.

Unwanted Stories

As we rounded the corner, Pinku pointed out the house to me. We had just come from a village in Pali, not that far from Falna, and a school where we had met with a group of girls who had now been attending regularly for a good few months. It was time to visit some of the homes where Pinku admitted she was struggling. This confident young woman had been on one of my first colleague Vikram's team for a little over a year, and was proving to be one of our most tenacious team members. It was her fourth visit to try and enrol Prachi. I was to meet Prachi for the first time.

I felt like she saw us coming. Sarita, Prachi's elegant mother, was standing at her doorstep, a baby hoisted onto her hip, wearing a beautiful, full floral ghaghra and a tight-fitting, faded choli. The baby fiddled with the ochre-yellow dupatta that obscured Sarita's eyes, but all the same I knew she was checking me out as we slowly entered the house. I admit I started to feel a knot in my stomach, anticipating a difficult conversation, and the expectation of the team was high.

We had had some success enrolling girls in this village, but there were still a few families left who were persistent in their refusal to send their girls to school, and Prachi was one of them.

At least eleven girls were now going to the village school, and I had loved meeting them in the morning while joining in some of their lessons. The task at hand was about persuasion. We were invited in and Pinku and I hesitantly sat down in her yard behind the house. Sarita was busy doing a myriad of chores. She had a baby hammock hanging on a small frame. A goat was tied to the side while her jet-black lamb was running around freely. Prachi was also there, picking stones from lentils and cleaning them in a bowl of cloudy water before they could be cooked. She was close to thirteen years old, had been pulled out of school and we wanted to convince Sarita to enrol her back in.

That was the first time that Sarita had met me. She knew the team well and the team knew Sarita, but Pinku thought that my coming from Mumbai and sitting with her myself might just help—perhaps a new face, a new story might help change Sarita's mind. She was polite and welcoming, but she already muttered to Pinku that we were wasting her time. Pinku pointed at me, encouraging me to step forward:

'*Ye Safeena-ji hain, Sarita. Ye inhi ki sanstha hai. Ye Mumbai se aayi hai, aapse aur Prachi se milne!* [This is Safeena-ji, Sarita. Its her organization. She has come from Mumbai to meet you and Prachi!]' With her words she tried to elevate my importance.

With my hands clasped together as if in prayer, I bowed my head slightly and carried on where Pinku had left off.

'Sarita-ji, I am so happy to meet you—thank you so much for inviting me to your home!' I was not sure if Sarita felt she had 'invited' me into her home, but nonetheless I wanted to thank her and say how happy I was to meet her.

I immediately launched into an explanation of why I had come. I told her what we believed in—that education is every girl's right and that every girl should have the opportunity to go to school. I explained what was on my mind and in my heart. Girls' education was so important. Every girl needed to study and deserved to have the same opportunities as a boy. Without an education, girls couldn't earn, they couldn't become independent and get ahead in life. And then I got to the point:

'We would really like you to enrol Prachi back in school. This is why we had come.' Sarita nodded at everything I said.

'I understand,' she politely responded. 'But school is not for Prachi,' she added in a more decisive tone.

I tried a little more and asked her even more directly: 'Wouldn't you like Prachi to learn to read? To maybe get a good job or set up a small business?' I speculated.

I could feel Sarita's frustration rising. Etiquette, however, prevented her from being rude to me. So after twenty minutes or so, Sarita scooped up Prachi's little sister, who was now crawling around her, turned the baby to face me, held her tiny hand in hers and made her wave goodbye to me. Back and forth she wiggled the baby's hand in hers.

'*Taa taa ... Aunty ko bye karo* [say bye to aunty]!' she implored her baby, and the little hand waved to and fro. She was signalling as strongly as she could that the conversation was over and she wanted us to leave.

Pinku interjected—she tried to explain that it was quite special for Sarita that I had visited her this time; she repeated how far I had come from. I was the leader of this NGO, she mentioned again. Her daughter's education was *that* important. But she was met with an awkward silence as Sarita placed the baby in the cradle and went back to her chores.

'Let's have a photo!' Pinku suggested before Sarita could get away, and we gathered together. Sarita cocked her head and smiled a wry kind of smile as I shuffled awkwardly next to her and posed for the camera. A smile that said—'This isn't going to work!'

I felt like I could hear what she was thinking—I could read it in her eyes. 'Even if you take my photo, I can't enrol Prachi in school. Take my photo, take a video, put me on TV—I won't change my mind.' I was convinced that this was what was going through her mind. As I moved to sit back down again. She beamed a big smile in my direction again. This was all in good humour, and yet decisive. She was adamant. Her mind was made up.

By now Pinku and I had given up trying to change Sarita's thinking. We felt this was pretty much a dead-end conversation. However, I had to wait for Vikram to pick me up so I asked if we could wait there in her home for some more time. Sarita, relieved that the conversation had ended, nodded and we hung back in her yard. I sat beside Prachi and could not resist playing with the little lamb, who was interested in chewing everything from my shawl to my notebook.

With one hand on the lamb, I turned to Prachi.

'Do you miss school?' I enquired. She said no, she didn't like school and had left after a fight. I was a little surprised and asked her what the fight was about.

'I was always fighting with the other children as they made fun of me,' Prachi explained as she nonchalantly cleaned the lentils.

'Why did they make fun of you?' I probed.

'Because I did badly in school.' Then suddenly she pushed her hair back and showed me her ear. The ear was closed. It was deformed.

'I couldn't hear very well from that side and so they all made fun of me. I kept on fighting with them and finally I left the school swearing I would never go back.'

As I stroked the lamb and listened, I think Prachi started to warm to me, but I still left feeling dejected. She would still not go to school and nothing I had said had worked. Vikram came and picked me up and we went to another home.

He was one of the first people I had hired when we started work in Pali. He had responded to our need to hire someone to work on data analysis, but he soon became my keenest ally. Today, he leads our national team.

When we arrived at the next house for our visit, there was only the father at home with his daughter Kirti. Vikram walked in and greeted him: 'Ram Ram, bhaiya.' He introduced himself with a namaste, a '*Kaise hain?* [How are you?]' and a knowledgeable enquiry about this season's harvest.

'The rains have been so good this year, I bet you will have had good returns from your harvest!' he speculated in a knowing way.

We noticed the peanuts laid out just in front of the house to be cleaned, so Vikram commented again on how well they had turned out that year. I wondered when he was going to start to ask about the little girl we had seen outside tending to the goats, but Vikram continued with more questions about how the peanuts were grown, where they were sold, and what else the father did beyond farming.

'Labouring,' the man replied, adding that he, his wife and his daughter Kirti would be leaving shortly for the building site. Vikram finally had an in.

'Will she just spend the rest of her life working? Let her study a bit too, na?' he said.

We, of course, knew all along we wanted to ask about Kirti—we knew she was not going to school. We knew we wanted to direct the conversation around to school, but Vikram knew the way to do this. As with Sarita, the response he got at first was not positive. The father, in a polite but detached manner, said that he was not interested. Education may be a good thing but he did not think he needed it for his daughter; she was only going to get married and settle down in another home.

Vikram agreed with him: it was true that most girls would marry and settle down. But then he went on to recount a deeply personal story of his own sister, who had grown up in Pali just twenty-five kilometres from where we were, a story that he thought they might relate to.

His younger sister, Vikram explained, was educated up to graduation level. She married a man from a family of landowners, who did not really have any other skill or income beyond what they earned from their land. After a dispute ensued, his sister and her husband fell out with his family and were estranged from their in-laws. They had no income or prior training to fall back on. And to make things worse, her husband was diagnosed with epilepsy so it was even more difficult for him to find work. Therefore, the burden to earn fell on Vikram's sister's shoulders. But here was the thing: because of her education, she was able to start a career as an anganwadi[1] worker. Without her education her whole family would have suffered greatly with the unexpected illness in the family. Health shocks are very often a major cause of families falling into or back into poverty. Vikram explained what his father always said when recalling this story: 'When my daughter married, I paid her dowry. *Sabse keemti dahej jo maine usse diya woh thi uski shiksha* [The most valuable dowry I gave was actually her education],' Vikram quoted his father in a serious, proud voice.

Kirti's father nodded, obviously taking in the whole story, but he then had his own questions—stress-testing Vikram's story and its authenticity. Which caste was Vikram's family from? Where did he stay? Which district? Which block? How much land had they owned? 'Are these people like me?' I could sense him wanting to ask. 'Is this story relevant for me, for my family, for Kirti?' He then paused, and after a brief thought, concluded: 'Come back next time and let me see the form.' The father was quite matter-of-fact in his statement, as if nothing much had changed.

But everything had. With this one simple statement so much had changed, and it was clear that Vikram had opened the door to a conversation. Now the work really began, but this was the moment we knew something shifted—Vikram's conversation had been a turning point. Dowry was a currency that this father had understood. Dowry held a value he recognized. There was cultural resonance. It took Vikram and the team another three visits before Kirti was finally enrolled in school. The form was shared with the father, and Vikram took him to meet the headmaster and see the school for himself. The rather aloof grandmother I had sat with, who was also somewhat dismissive of her granddaughter's need for education, had also needed persuading. But in the end, she was convinced. Where I had felt the door closing in my face with Sarita and Prachi, Vikram had succeeded in cracking it open, and the result spoke for itself.

That evening I reflected on those two visits. What could I learn from those encounters? Those two attempts at enrolment? What were the elements that led to failure in one household and the beginnings of success in the other? What was at the root of changing a mindset, a school of thought? What did it take? Vikram was local, from the same district, he spoke the dialect. He took the time to build a rapport with the father. He did not talk *at* him, about why girls *should* be educated, but demonstrated the value of girls' education through a deeply authentic and relatable personal experience. Vikram used the right story.

I felt I was an outsider when I thought through my attempts and how I could be perceived. But it was not just that Vikram was an insider, it was also how he built a relationship with this father. What could I have done differently with Sarita? Even if I had been a local, there were things I should have done differently. I should have listened to her and to Prachi. I should have asked more questions. I realized I had talked *at* Sarita. I had launched into my story and my opinions, and not really given either of them an opportunity to share their story. I had not appreciated what their silence and polite smiles had really meant.

We debriefed as a team to see what we could do in Prachi's case. We decided that we would go back and speak with Sarita about getting Prachi evaluated at the government hospital for her hearing, and then if she could get a disability certificate given the situation with her ear, she would be eligible for a state pension. We had to restart our conversation with Sarita and Prachi and see if that helped bring her back to school. If not, access to this scheme would still provide Prachi with a regular income and help her sustain herself financially.

I had of course made a large number of home visits before that day. We were in our first year of operations and I went out a lot with the team, but that day was different. The contrast between mine and Vikram's approaches had never been so clear to me, and I had learnt important lessons. For a mindset change to happen you have to *show* the value of an education, not just tell. I was slowly starting to realize the power of storytelling in challenging mindsets and changing minds. Telling a story can connect people. Through a story you can share perspectives, and more than anything a story can evoke feelings and encourage empathy. But this must be done as part of building a relationship, investing time and effort in creating a rapport, listening and learning, and not just approaching it as a transactional exercise. The story has to have a local context and come with an authentic, relevant message.

The next question was: How would we take this to larger audiences?

Clothes Speak Volumes

> 'Her future is to get married and have children. She can learn all that at home.'
>
> 'What is the point of sending her to school?'
>
> 'An education will only spoil her and she will not follow her culture.'

I had heard statements like these over and over again while visiting girls' families at their homes, but this was not something I had heard in more public settings. Apart from individual meetings with parents and families, we also started to conduct village level meetings. Word would go out to the village leadership a couple of weeks in advance and we would collaborate in getting a critical mass of the community together in one place. I remember one particularly large meeting where there must have been around 200 people. It felt like a fair! People were sitting in a large circle. There were men on nearby roofs and children in trees swinging their legs and watching the proceedings with curiosity and excitement.

Vijayalakshmi, one of our most charismatic block officers, was running the meeting. She welcomed everyone warmly, introducing all the key stakeholders who were there, from the sarpanch to the headmasters and other influencers of the community. Then she proceeded to speak of the number of girls who were not in school in the village and made a plea to their parents for all of them to be enrolled. While she was speaking very passionately, I noticed a young man leaning on a bicycle looking restless and chewing paan. While Vijayalakshmi was still addressing the crowd, he interrupted, 'We don't send our girls to schools because we know what happens when they do.' He smirked and carried on chewing, the paan muffling his words.

'*Kya hota hai*? What happens?' asked Vijayalakshmi with a tone of feigned ignorance. She knew what he was likely to say— it was something she had no doubt heard many times before. But still she gave him the opportunity to explain.

The young man turned his head away from the crowd, spat loudly and sprayed blood-red paan and saliva across the parched ground. 'They wear short clothes and have love marriages!' he proclaimed, this time with an empty mouth and a lot more clarity.

There was silence. Everyone was looking at Vijayalakshmi to see her reaction. It immediately crossed my mind that a majority of those at the meeting were probably thinking the same thing as this brazen young man. They were just not ready to be the first to say it out loud. I ran through a couple of responses in my head trying to frame the way I might react, but I drew a blank. I had no idea what to say. This time I really felt like an outsider; sitting amongst so many people with some obvious tension. The children continued to swing their legs to and fro, lightening the situation a little. Surely nothing serious like a fight could happen with so many youngsters around? But I wasn't sure. My eyes bounced from the young man to Vijayalakshmi and back again and then rested on her as she scanned the crowd, identified the headmaster and drew him into the conversation. She addressed him confidently but tried to show an air of bafflement: 'Sir,' she began, gesturing across the crowd. '*Aapki ek beti hai na?* [You have a daughter, right?]'

'Yes,' replied the headmaster. He did not look that much older than the paan-chewing man. But he was calm and authoritative.

'And you educated your daughter, right, sir?'

'I did,' confirmed the headmaster, nodding emphatically.

'So is she wearing short clothes and running away from home to get a love marriage? Are you teaching all these things in your school, sir?' She pointed beyond the crowd to the school building.

At first there was a hush, and in the deafening silence I realized I had been holding my breath! And then everyone in the meeting let out a raucous laugh and the tension was immediately diffused. The headmaster got up and gave the young man a sharp scolding 'for talking rubbish'. He explained to everyone how school was for studying and learning languages, mathematics, physical education and all the other subjects. What this young man was referring to were cultural values which were learnt in the home and family. He firmly put the insolent young man in his place and convinced the community that they must send their girls to school. He also offered to give admission right on the spot at the meeting for all those who agreed.

That day I learnt another valuable lesson, this time from Vijayalakshmi. I learnt the importance of local role models and influencers in driving a mindset change. She had drawn the village leaders in and made them lead this conversation. Her careful questions of the headmaster had ensured that the message came from him, not her. Of course, we understood that cultural values can also be learnt or reaffirmed at school as well as in the family, but the headmaster's argument that day was just what we had needed in the moment. Vijayalakshmi rightly knew that the people were far more likely to listen to the village leader and school headmaster than they were to us. So, she had invited them to respond to this man. And, thereby, ensured that the community came up with their own answers. There had been no 'telling' by us; she had merely facilitated the right people and the right message. While I had sat there trembling, unable to think how to react to this young man and his rigid mindset, Vijayalakshmi had turned everything around. This was true community ownership of our mission and I began to see the power of local stories in one village after another.

Beneath the Veil

Madhuri stood up in front of the large crowd which had gathered in front of the school building. She was veiled, but peeped out of her pallu to look out over a crowd of some forty villagers. To her right, the older men sat cross-legged, clothed in white, and the younger men sat behind them. To her left and further back, the ladies joined the meeting, all veiled, and the children sat among them. This was a particularly conservative village and, yet, unusually, they had a female sarpanch, Madhuri Kholi.

Madhuri started off with a question: 'Why aren't your girls going to school?'

A cacophony of voices answered, with an overwhelming message, 'Who's going to do all the housework then? *Phir ghar ka kaam kaun karega?*'

There were indignant laughs. Men and women alike gestured at the floor that lay between Madhuri and them, as if to point out that it needed sweeping. This was also what many parents said to us. Time and again. They said they had no choice. There was no one else. Girls had to stay home. Who would look after the siblings? Who would collect the water? Who would prepare the food? Wash the clothes? Housework was a constant repeated theme—a leitmotif of sorts. But Madhuri was adamant and respectfully challenged them all. 'It's not about the work. You can manage somehow. Today, tomorrow and the rest of your life there is going to be work to do at home. Regardless, it's important to educate our girls, *humari balikaon ko padhana bahut zaroori hai.*'

Then she gestured to one of the girls, Swati, who had been a recent dropout but was now back in the classroom. The seven-year-old stood up and confidently recited the English alphabet, all twenty-six letters. Grins stretched across every face in the meeting—it was impossible for the gathered adults not to acknowledge this little girl's effort.

'That's my granddaughter,' one of the older gentlemen, Hitan, announced. Hitan's granddaughter knew English now, in a village where no one understood the language! There was joy in her eyes at the potential of her knowledge.

'Hitan is shedding a tear, he is so proud!' a woman cried out, almost mockingly.

He drew a crumpled hanky from his pocket and wiped his cheek as Madhuri questioned him, 'You won't pull her out of school again now, will you, Hitan-ji?'

'I won't,' responded her proud grandfather.

Madhuri was smart. She had celebrated Hitan in front of his community, and in doing so had created an ally for herself. Someone respected by the village had made a public agreement to keep his granddaughter in school. Madhuri then went on to share her own story.

'If I wasn't educated I wouldn't have been elected to this role of sarpanch,' Madhuri explained.

Madhuri was part of the village leadership, and what she had so wisely done was build public accountability to her mission, and this group meeting was helping. Hitan, an elder but not a leader, had spoken out. He had made an open commitment to education in front of his neighbours and friends, and the hope was that peer pressure might help him to keep his granddaughter in school and at the same time build aspiration through little Swati for other girls in the village, for other families. In a village where no one spoke English, she had built the credibility of school and education through little Swati reciting her ABCs. It was one thing getting the village leaders on our side, the next was getting the full village, the community members themselves, to acknowledge the role they played and the responsibility they needed to take for girls to go to school.

Madhuri had certainly made the right impact in the meeting—using the right tone, hitting the right note, using the right examples. She championed the girls, and yet respected the local customs. Beneath her veil she conformed, but at the same time pushed the village to change.

Larger village meetings were getting our messages heard at scale and both leaders and the village at large were starting to change their minds and build a village-wide commitment. There was immense power in mobilizing *everyone* to make a case for girls' education. Through their own examples they created the space for mindset change in their communities as we started to realize the power of story-telling. Our job was to create the right platforms, and then it was all about stories being told so that *new stories* could be written for the girls.

Plays that Perform the Perils

And so this is how we slowly started to change the story for girls. At doorsteps and in meetings, we harnessed stories from each village to clearly illustrate the importance of education, and the importance of girls. To challenge mindsets and change both beliefs and behaviours we had to show and illustrate as clearly as possible the perils of illiteracy and the injustice of excluding girls from school. We had to find narratives to help parents loosen their tight grip on the past, on culture, on traditions, and visualize a better future for their daughters.

We listened. We heard stories and we began to share those stories at every opportunity. Those stories became plays, and eventually those plays slowly started to communicate the messages we wanted to be heard.

One such play was being performed at a ratri chaupal (evening meeting). In some of the villages it was pointless going door to door during the day as most of the parents were working. We started to arrange evening meetings and make them a little more sociable and engaging by putting on plays. The sun would set at almost the same time every day in Rajasthan the whole year round. As the sky turned a dirty pink, the cicadas struck up their chorus, and the air became thick with the smell of wood-burning stoves and the evening meal. We tended to hold our meetings at around 8 p.m. It was cool, everyone was fed, and with the light of their mobile phone batteries, the community would find their way from their homes to the courtyard by the school.

On one particular evening when I joined such a meeting, the stage was set. The team had laid out a large blue tarpaulin on the wide road outside the village shop and the sarpanch's house. It was very dark, but three bright light bulbs were strung across the street and a lantern dangled in front of the screen we had erected, making an odd shadow across the film screen. Educate Girls posters also hung from the electricity wires like washing on the line, enclosing the space almost like a tent, and at the same time reinforcing our message.

The village members sat in groups and the 'actors' took their position just in front of the screen. One field coordinator was acting as Alka, a mother who was missing her son.

Alpesh (Alka's son in the play) was sixteen and had struggled to earn enough money in the village, so he had moved out of the district in search of work. He would occasionally write to his mother to keep her abreast of his movements, but as she couldn't read, she would rely on someone reading his letters to her. (This was all narrated to the audience by the budding NGO-workers-turned-actors.) A new letter arrived and Alka was seen waving it and looking for someone to help her understand it. Alka walked around the audience with the letter in her hand, asking for help to read it. Eventually, Alka found someone to help her, but she too admitted she was only able to read a little and couldn't fully understand what the letter said. Another actor took the letter, pulled it close to his face and demonstrated difficulty in reading it.

'*Aaj … mar … gaya …*' her friend read out haltingly. 'Yes, that's it—*Aaj mar gaya.*' As those words sank in, Alka's blood ran cold. Today he died. Her only son, her beautiful boy, had gone in search of work, been away for three months and today he had died? Distraught, she snatched the letter and ran off.

I knew the story already as we had discussed it as a team, but even I was moved by the emotional performance. The play continued, with Alka now shrouded in white acting out the last rites for her son, mourning. The actors left the stage.

'A month later …' they announced.

There was a knock on the door, and Alka, still in mourning, opened it. It was Alpesh, her son! She dropped whatever was in her hands. 'My son,' she screamed, acting like she had seen a ghost. 'How is this possible? How come you are alive? Your letter said "*Aaj mar gaya*"!'

'*Ma, Ma, main Ajmer gaya tha!*' said Alpesh. 'The letter did not say "*Aaj mar gaya*", it said "*Ajmer gaya*"! [I went to the town of Ajmer],' he explained.

Her son was back. She had thought he was dead, but Alpesh had been to Ajmer in search of work. He was back from the dead. The gathered crowd fell about in hysterics. Death is no laughing matter, but the team used this rather extreme but true story to illustrate the perils of illiteracy. 'We need our girls to read!' was the overwhelming message.

The other example that night was the story of a woman, Anu, who had an eye infection. Anu went to the doctor to show him her eye, and he prescribed some eye ointment in a small yellow tube that she had to apply several times a day. Anu went home and after some time asked her daughter-in-law Sita, '*Bahu, zara meri peeli tube lekar ana. Aankh mein dalni hain.*' [Daughter-in-law, bring me the ointment in the yellow tube to put in my eye].'

Again, our field team took on the roles of the woman and her daughter-in-law. They had two different yellow tubes that they dramatically placed on a makeshift table. Anu beckoned to Sita to fetch her the eye ointment. Sita approached the table and picked up a yellow tube, squinting at the writing on it, obviously unable to read the name or application instructions. She pretended to put what she thought was the eye ointment into her mother-in-law's eyes. The next moment, Anu was reeling in pain and Sita was distraught as she realized she has put a highly toxic tyre glue into her mother-in-law's eye instead of the eye ointment. The two tubes were held aloft. The reaction of the crowd this time was less raucous and more shocked and uncomfortable, as Anu was rendered blind. Again, this was all based on a true story. The point was again driven home about how critical it was for our girls to be able to read. Literacy could be a matter of life or death.

The Negative Loop

The plays were highly effective and a great way for our team members to communicate to a larger audience in one sitting but also rehearse the arguments and negotiations they often made on doorsteps to one family at a time. On another evening, when I joined a session, two highly effective arguments were made on stage by Jaspreet and Gauri, two Educate Girls team members.

'My wife can only be seen by a female doctor!' Jaspreet was playing the role of a determined husband seeking to 'protect' his wife and have her examined only by a female doctor. An understandable position for us city dwellers, who have a choice when we want to see a doctor. Most practices or hospitals have more than one doctor and a mix of male and female professionals. In rural India, this is not the case.

'Sir, until more girls are allowed to go to school and study at college, there won't be any female doctors to look after your wife!' Gauri continued, playing herself. 'Can I ask if your daughter goes to school?'

'I won't send my daughter to school unless and until the teacher is a woman!' Jaspreet retorted, acting as a defiant father.

'Sir, again, until more girls are allowed to go to school and study at college, there won't be any female teachers for your village and for your daughter,' Gauri explained in a resigned tone.

Pointing out the negative loop of denying a girl her education, the hope was that the point would be made, and that the audience would see the bind this father was getting himself into. Although across India, there is by and large gender parity in the teaching profession at the primary level, in the most remote parts of the country village teachers are much more likely to be men.[2] And until this missing generation of girls are allowed to go to school and complete twelve years of education, there will be no female doctors to attend to the women as they fall ill, and there will be no female teachers to break the cycle of illiteracy.

Real-life examples of the need for education are one of the strongest levers for change. In these real stories and short sketches, the audience was being shown how short-sighted so much of this mindset is. The mindset of the burden, the mindset of the liability, the mindset of the girl that needs shutting away, 'protecting' from the world. To counter all these narratives, we need stories that paint a picture of a much brighter future through the legal protection of girls' rights and education. And this is how we turn the page.

Stories of Solutions

'I get up around 5 a.m. and collect the water. Once I am home by 6 a.m. I start to prepare the food and then help my brother bathe and get ready for school. I sweep and tidy the house and then if everything is ready I go to school with my brother. Otherwise, if I still have some chores to do, like laundry, I am late for school.' This is what Neeti told me when I met her a year after we had helped enrol her into school. Neeti had started off going to school part-time, but over the course of the year she had worked out how to manage all her chores before and after school hours. However, she was tired. This was not an easy situation. But parents do get used to the new routine and start to see the benefits of education over time.

To create a contrast with the stories of the perils of illiteracy, we also shared stories of young girls who have thrived through education, stories of practical solutions that have been implemented by parents who have sent their girls to school. Parents want to hear stories of families like themselves, who have managed to cope once their daughters have gone to school. Sometimes, it is a philosophical or ideological debate that is won. But sometimes it is purely practical. We tried anything and everything that might work.

When families are paralysed by the fear that 'the work won't get done' we are fighting two battles: the battle against poverty and the circumstances that put families into situations where they need everyone to work and earn. 'Who will look after the goats?' 'Who will run the shop?' 'Who will clean the house and look after the baby sibling so both parents can earn?' As well as the battle of patriarchy that dictates that this is all a daughter's job, not a son's. Our team strategizes and helps find ways, and often we have to negotiate and take it slow. Parents and girls who have never been to school need time to get used to the idea. Girls need to get used to going to school, sitting in the classroom. Parents need to get used to the fact that their girls are not home all day, every day. Generally, schools are open to children coming for part of the day so they can get used to the change and if necessary balance their work and lessons. Invariably when this happens, families slowly realize they can cope and the girls are often allowed to then go to school full-time. For many girls the reality is such that they still have to get the work done and only then go to school. Going to school is not an easy path when all the odds are stacked against you.

The Parallel Lives of Goats and Girls

This was a solution we used for Meenu eventually. We were again at a village meeting where Chandan, one of the fathers, stood up and with an air of pride explained the changes he had made in his household to accommodate his daughter's wish to go to school.

'We do need more help to graze the goats, but we manage. If Meenu goes to school, she will have an opportunity to make something of herself, to get a job and a good husband,' he paused, perhaps recollecting some of the things the Educate Girls volunteer had explained about the injustices of child marriage. 'But in time, maybe when she is twenty,' he clarified.

The ambition for a 'good' marriage remained. Meenu's agency was perhaps not yet her own, but the goat-herding barrier had been overcome; goats were no longer her 'reason for being'. Meenu's father aspired for something more for her. Here was a father who had changed his mind.

But it hadn't always been this way. When we first met Chandan two years ago the school was 'too far'. When I arrived at their home it was late. The grasshoppers' rattle had begun, the heat had been removed from the sun, and as it disappeared into the embrace of the valley the shadows chased us across the village. We had missed Meenu's parents every time we visited the village, so that time we went in the evening. Seema, her mother, had spent all day in the nearby town selling bundles of wheat. Chandan reached home a little later, and just as I asked where Meenu was, I heard the discordant chime of the goat's bells as they returned from the hill.

Every day Meenu covered a good 5 kilometres with the goats. During the summers, it was harder to find a patch to graze. Her days were hard and long, but Meenu also enjoyed being out in the fields. Except for when the heatwave came. And recently the heat seemed harsher and the wave longer.

After a number of years in the fields with her goats, and her goats' parents, Meenu knew them as well as her own sisters! 'This is Bakasura-Bakri, she has a long neck!' she laughed, expecting me to remember that Bakasura was the crane demon. 'This is Balarama, and the white one is Banasura. This one is Bhadra—she is the mother—and this is Bhishmaka.'

I was quite taken aback that Meenu's goats were all named after characters from the Bhagavata Purana. No one in her family could read. But stories were passed down from generation to generation, recounted not read, and Meenu remembered them by repeating them a lot, mostly to her goats.

Eventually, I asked, 'Why does Meenu not go to school?'

'*School bahut door hai* [School is too far],' her parents explained. Meenu was eight years old, but had not yet set foot in the local school. They were right, their home only just belonged to this village, it was a 2-kilometre walk along the road that led out of the village and climbed the first elevation of the ridge where Chandan and Seema lived. We listened and nodded. There was a hint of fear and an air of protection in her voice as Seema continued: 'It doesn't seem safe to have Meenu walk all that way every day. *Surakshit nahin hai* [It's not safe]. There aren't any other children who live this far from the school.' But Meenu walked more than 5 kilometres a day with the goats. She scaled the dusty hillock behind their home—not alone as she had the goats for company, but alone, really. She went to the river to wash clothes, she went to the well to collect water. Meenu also had to go to the fields to defecate; there was no bathroom at their home.

Safety was another school of thought. The default position when explaining school absence was 'distance', 'safety'—'*School door hai*'. But we had to work out a way to challenge this constructively. Avoiding shame and criticism, pointing out capabilities, allaying fear and building confidence. A girl's absence from the school register was so often explained through an insurmountable problem. But it was noticeable how this was just not the case for boys. Whereas the default position for girls was that education was too difficult. Distance was rarely an issue for a boy. Safety was not a concern. School was not too far for their sons. But for their daughters, it was different.

It took us pointing out with encouragement and empathy that Meenu's daily commute with her goats was at least twice as far as school. That the road into the village was actually a lot safer than scaling the hill on her own. After the first few hundred yards, it even turned from track to concrete. Slowly, we chipped away at the barrier. Eventually, we unearthed the fact that no one else was there to look after the goats if

Meenu was in school. But again we listened. It wasn't every day that Seema was not around for the goats. The job could be shared.

'How about we start by enrolling Meenu in school and she can go for half a day?' For Seema and Chandan to go from having a full-time goat herder to nothing was a step too far, too fast. We suggested a solution where Meenu attended school in the mornings, but by mid-afternoon she could take the goats. As the weeks rolled by, the family found ways. Meenu balanced her home work with helping out, her education slowly became a priority, and a year on Chandan was at the village meeting mentioning his story—Meenu's story—to influence some of his neighbours to send their girls to school.

The Worries of a Widow

We perhaps stayed a little long at the school one morning a few days later, and we had nearly visited all the houses on our list before the sun decided to halt us in our tracks. Exhausted, dripping with sweat, we took cover in the shade of the school and recuperated with warm water from our bottles and energy from our tiffins. But after a couple of hours in the shade, we set out again by around 3 p.m., determined to reach Anilbhai's house. Anilbhai had died eighteen months ago from some fever, we were told. It was often hard to understand the cause of death in many cases as medical professionals were rarely involved and many, many life-threatening ailments included a fever. It was likely he had died of malaria, but it could have been dysentery, it could have been dengue. Whatever the diagnosis, Anilbhai had died, leaving behind a wife, five daughters and his ageing mother.

When we talk about 'going to the margins', I experienced this in its most visceral sense that day. In the village meeting, they had pointed to the hut across the fields and the tiny temple. It had been marked on the 'not to scale' map by a little purple arrow at the very edge of the paper, pointing south-west with the distance '2 km' written next to it. So we walked 2 kilometres, following the map, past the wayside shrine that had a fresh string of marigolds and a smouldering clay diya (lamp). The late Anilbhai's home was on the edge of a forest, and in the absence of schemes, in the absence of work, in the absence of Anilbhai, it was the forest that now sustained his family. This was to be our last household visit that day, as I found it incredibly hard to tear myself away.

Anilbhai's widow, Shanti, was once an energetic woman. She plucked a faded photo from behind a mirror that was hung on the wall, one of those stiff, garlanded wedding photos. But the couple looked unusually happy. In most of such photos, the lack of love and the forced nature of the arranged marriage was only too obvious, but Shanti looked quite radiant, quite plump. That was over a decade ago, she sighed. Since then, Shanti had had five daughters, who had to this day never set foot in a school. She had lost a husband, and a lot of weight.

We had been in conversation for a good hour before Shanti tried to serve me tea and I tried to change the subject swiftly. No tea was made, and I just about felt comfortable asking her: 'How many meals do you have every day,

Shanti?' Not wanting to embarrass her, but wanting to really understand her situation.

'Once a day. We eat once a day.'

She explained that she and her daughters were able to forage some food from the woods, and beyond that they relied on rations. But none of this made for three meals a day. Her shrivelled mother-in-law had to be carried out of the hut in the morning, out of the sun and into the shade every hour or so as the sun moved, then back into the hut in the evening. Shanti had to do all of this with seven mouths to feed and no end to this cycle in sight.

'*School hum jaise logon ke lie nahin hai.* People like us can't afford to go to school. School is not for families like ours.' Shanti was adamant.

'But, Shanti', I implored, 'your girls can have a hot meal every day at school, and it's free.'

I don't think she quite understood what I was saying. No one had ever taken the time to explain to Shanti that school was free and the midday meal was free.[3] By the end of the hour or so with Shanti, I saw a new glint in her eyes, a glimpse of the Shanti from her wedding photo. Her grief was perhaps lifting, she was beginning to see something positive for her girls and an escape from the trap. As we dragged ourselves away, we left the household a little lighter. There was of course still a long process to finally get the girls to school, but we left five girls excited at the prospect of school and a mother excited at the prospect of their lunch!

I again asked to visit Shanti two years later, when I returned to her block for a government meeting. I had been really keen to visit her once more as she had made such an impression on me. With raising five daughters on her own, I was keen to make sure she had the support she needed.

Her girls were all going to school. All five of them. What had changed Shanti's mind, I wondered. 'Manjola didi was so persistent,' Shanti recalled, explaining her meeting with the Educate Girls volunteer. 'But I had a fight on my hands. Anilbhai's mother, meri saas [mother-in-law] was adamant that the girls should stay at home even when I explained about the midday meals. "What will the community think if the girls are walking to school every day—it's so far! They will bring shame on the family, crossing the village in front of the village youth!"' Shanti mimicked the old lady's intonation, her outrage, her indignation. The very idea that a girl's grandmother would stand in the way of her girls' education was a shock, but this was nothing we hadn't seen before.

'But when I became a widow, I realized how vulnerable we were. I am illiterate and can only work in the fields. What chance did I have to give my girls a better life if I couldn't access even the basics? Manjola didi got to know us and realized that I wasn't drawing my widow's pension. I wasn't aware of it.' Not being able to read is like not being able to see half the world, maybe more than half, I thought to myself as Shanti spoke.

'Manjola didi told me the story of a widow in the next village, who was not only able to draw her pension, but had gone back to school and qualified as an anganwadi worker. That's what I want for my girls. And I think it is what Anilbhai would have wanted too! Being widowed doesn't have to be the end. Deepti, my eldest, is now teaching me to write.'

And with that she picked up a stick and carefully wrote her name in the dry earth—SH AA N TI. 'See?' she told me proudly.

Turning the Page

The idea that a girl is a liability, that the journey to school is not safe, that girls should stay at home and prepare for marriage, the spectre of a love marriage—this is all a school of thought and one that has to be challenged. The main barriers driving this mindset can be divided into two clear categories: poverty and patriarchy. When the barrier is a patriarchal mindset, you have to build and drive home the importance of girls' education. You have to show how girls' education makes a difference in a hyperlocal context. When the barrier is poverty, as we saw in Shanti's case, then you have to ensure you support the family with knowledge and the skills to access social protection schemes to help build resilience and room for girls to be able to go to school and then eventually, hopefully, break that cycle of economic hardship.

What we are talking about here is shifting mindsets, and the 'process' for that is through deep human connection. Active listening, authentic empathy and shared vulnerability. We realized that this was not about facts, it was about emotional engagement. It was personal, not theoretical, and that's why the team was so important to our ability to change both hearts and minds.

4

Learning Who Should Lead

'Go to the people. Live with them. Learn from them. Love them. Start with what they know. Build with what they have. But with the best leaders, when the work is done, the task accomplished, the people will say, "We have done this ourselves."'

—Lao Tzu, *Tao Te Ching*

But who should be that person to listen and share? The 'what' needed to be done was perhaps the easier part of our journey to navigate. As I mentioned mindset change was my guiding light at the core of *what* we needed to do. But finding *who* was the right person to drive this work forward and make these deep connections with families, parents and girls and then influence the changes we wanted to see for girls, was certainly a harder undertaking. In the next couple of years, up until 2012, we were again looking and learning.

The Warnings Land

I heard a loud thud, and something landed on the ground just ahead of us. Dust puffed up like a small cloud and stopped us in our tracks. I recoiled in shock.

'Arre, sorry, I should have warned you!' Vikram explained. 'He usually misses, but once or twice he did manage to hit me on the shoulder!'

We were quite far from the school building where we had parked after reaching a village in Rani block. We had arrived a few hours ago and were slowly walking around, making note of the struggles of its residents. It was essentially a patchwork of hamlets, loosely knitted together with winding dust tracks that criss-crossed the hillside. And as we walked and walked, we passed a pile of damp clothes beside a partly dried-up pond and two small burnt pits that Vikram explained were for brewing the desi liquor. He was native to this area and could read the land, like 'reading between the lines' in his favourite book.

Just ahead, I could make out a cluster of three huts and a charpai, half in and half out of the shade created by the overhang of one of the tin roofs. A skinny black-and-white dog lay stretched out in front of one of the shacks. Since Pooja's mother died in 2007, her father, Ram, struggled to cope with the loss of his wife and the sudden doubling of parental responsibility. He took to drinking and, as a consequence, also lost his income. Pooja was the youngest of three girls. When you are born the third, you know. You know that your parents were desperate for a boy, for their last chance at a son to carry the family name. A third attempt in a community like Ram's is a sure sign of son preference.

Ram no longer wanted to engage with the world, and every time Vikram had as much as approached Ram's home, a large stone was lobbed in his direction. Depending on his state of inebriation, some days he hit his target. Most days the stone fell short, as it did that day. But the warning landed.

It wasn't the first warning either. We wanted to speak to families about their girls and the village school, but we were not welcome. Questions whirled around the village, sometimes whispers, sometimes shouts. Who were we? Why were we so interested in the girls? Were we the government? Were we the police? To attract less attention to ourselves, we started leaving our vehicles at the main road and entered the village either on foot or on a bike. But even that was problematic. A few days earlier, I had offered to sit on the back of Vikram's motorcycle to visit a far-off village, not dissimilar to this one. I sat side-saddle, shawl flapping behind me in the breeze and fingers tightly gripping the sides of the bike seat. Given my rigid posture, I could only look sideways as the countryside whisked past. Tree after tree.

When we arrived in the village, I jumped down from the bike, stretched my stiff neck, and no sooner had I straightened my clothes and tried unsuccessfully to tame my hair, we were immediately confronted by a group of curious members of the community. It would have been fine had Vikram been a relative of mine, but he wasn't. The men questioned us sharply. One waved a menacing-looking stick. We explained who we were, but were met with hostility. In traditional rural communities like this, a girl can only leave the house if she is veiled and accompanied by a male relative. With this as a norm, an 'expectation', to see a young woman on the back of a bike with a man who wasn't her relative or husband was unpalatable, setting a bad example and essentially just wrong. The mindset in this village towards girls was obvious from the very outset. We didn't get to open our mouths that day. We got back on the bike and left, knowing we had a lot to learn.

I began to get very disillusioned. Our mission was important. We cared deeply about the girls in these villages. We wanted to do the appropriate thing, be sensitive to the community yet still challenge rigid mindsets, but at every turn something wasn't quite right. Engaging with parents about their children's education wasn't as straightforward as you might have thought. The term 'being caught between a rock and a hard place' suddenly held a rather literal meaning for me, and I was certainly learning the hard way!

It was a surprise to us that many of these villages had never received a visit from a government official, let alone a social worker or an NGO representative. Outsiders just never came. Rumours spread that we had come looking for children to kidnap. Sometimes, it was our dress that was problematic—we needed to know what the appropriate attire was for a village visit and dress accordingly. Should we wear salwar-kameez or a saree? Should we be veiled? Sometimes, it was what we said—a misconstrued question, an uncomfortable line of enquiry. Sometimes, it was just our tone or our lack of knowledge of the local dialect. In one village, I had to hitch up my saree and run from a pack of furious dogs. In another, a man with pure rage in his eyes picked up his rifle.

It was clear that we weren't welcome, but was it the message or was it the messenger? At night I was kept awake trying to figure out what we were doing wrong. I lay there, staring at the shadows as they moved across the ceiling. But all I could see in my mind's eye were the faces of the girls and women we were trying to find. Vibha. Pooja. Prachi. Antimbala.

Back to Development Theory

With Antimbala, with every last girl we were trying to find at the forefront of my mind, I spoke to others in the development sector and they said:

> 'Listen to the elders.'
> 'Engage and find the influencers in the village.'
> 'Persuade the *mature* members of a community to advocate with you.'
> 'Seek out the older generation!'

I went back to the books.

This wasn't really the strategy I wanted to follow. I wanted to learn by *doing*, not by reading *again*. I had read the development theory books before, when I had started working in community health in South America. At that time, I combined the practical with the theoretical. But my recent failures and anxiety led me to conclude that I obviously needed to refresh my ideas. We knew we had to change mindsets through telling stories, and I wanted to see results and see girls in school. But something wasn't working.

So to break through this impasse, I reviewed the theory and concluded I would do what the books said: I would seek out the older generation.

And there he was at my next village meeting, sitting at the very edge of the school veranda. He had positioned himself right in the arc of the early afternoon sun that made his pristine white turban glow; everyone else was in the shade. And I was right in his line of sight as the meeting progressed. He was most certainly the most mature member of this community meeting: he was an elder.

The village had come together to discuss improvements to the parent–teacher association and to hear from our new team about the importance of girls' enrolment and how they could support getting girls into school. After the leader of the village group and my colleague Meena had addressed the audience, they invited me to say a few words. Meena had started with her own story of overcoming her family's traditional views of women to succeed at school, study and then work in the social sector. She had seen a lot in her career so far. Meena was in fact employee number one and had joined us as a field coordinator. When Vikram then joined, they complemented each other well. She was a hard act to follow today, but I scanned the room, caught the eye of the older man on the veranda and started to tell my story. I kept my eyes firmly fixed on him as my words began to flow. And much to my satisfaction, his large white turban nodded back and forth in all the right places. He fixated on me and endorsed everything I said with a knowing grin and a slow, appreciative nod. I knew my message was landing when his eyes began to glint with tears. My voice became more authoritative as I gained in confidence. I was putting community development theory into practice. Making inroads at last.

At the end of the meeting, I thought the next thing to do would be to speak to this man one on one to discuss next steps, so I made a beeline for him round the edge of the courtyard. If we had this elder on our side, I was sure we would make rapid progress with girls' enrolment in this village. I looked back towards Vikram and cocked my head to the side, indicating for him to come with me to speak to the elderly gentleman. But he was deep in conversation with Arjun, the head master, and almost seemed to be purposefully ignoring my cues. I looked at him again and gestured for him to hurry up. 'Now is our chance!' I thought to myself. The old man was obviously not fast on his feet, but I was afraid he might leave, as many from the meeting had started to do. To my irritation, however, Arjun continued to whisper in Vikram's ear, while the latter looked like he was suppressing a big laugh. Finally, Vikram looked in my direction, but he was still trying desperately to keep a straight face.

I could not wait anymore and marched towards him across the courtyard, so I could drag him away from whatever joke they were sharing. We had work to do! In a slightly curt tone of voice, I asked Vikram to accompany me. But he and Arjun looked at my face and burst out laughing.

'*Woh afeemchi hai!* Safeena-ji, please do not speak to Dhirendra. The old man is an opium smoker. He comes to this place every day, chews his opium and sits down in the sun like this. He is always here. It doesn't really matter what the meeting is about, what is said. He will always sit here basking in the sun, swaying on his haunches. He might look like he is listening to you and nodding, but I can assure you he hasn't taken anything in.' Tears were now rolling down Vikram's cheeks from all the effort not to laugh out loud and keep a straight face at my stupidity.

I was crestfallen; my newly gained, self-congratulatory confidence fell through the floor and I felt foolish, to say the least. There I was, thinking I knew it all, but I didn't know *this* village. No one from the outside did. It was only those from the village who knew Dhirendra and his ways.

Shortly after this experience, with my confidence still knocked, we visited another village for a similar meeting. Right at the back of the courtyard sat a similar-aged man to Dhirendra. His turban was not as brilliantly white as Dhirendra's and his dhoti and pyjamas were much worse for wear. He was puffing away on his hookah and had a large, menacing mole on his upper lip. He was, like Dhirendra, the oldest man in the group. But I had learnt my lesson. I commenced the meeting, engaging more broadly with the wider group, pretty much dismissing the smoky presence at the back of the audience.

As we finished talking with the group, Vikram immediately went over to the man at the back of the courtyard, and when I realized it I tried to catch his eye too, to question what on earth he was doing. I wasn't going to fall for this again. I perhaps expected a humorous wink from him, but instead Vikram cocked his head and gestured for me to come over. I assumed that Vikram was going to just pass the time of day with this man and then get back to the serious work, but he insisted I join him. I shrugged my shoulders to question what he was asking me to do, but then reluctantly went over.

Vikram already knew of Prabhu-ji, the village priest. Despite his appearance and demeanour, Vikram had been alerted to the fact that he was the key person we had to meet in this village. I assumed he was inebriated, but apparently he was thinking deeply. I judged him from his dress and assumed he was some dacoit, but instead I discovered he was, perhaps, the greatest champion for girls' education I was to meet in a while. Prabhu-ji, meaning 'master', 'Lord' or 'superior to the kings', was indeed a powerful man in the village. His temple was right across the road from the village school, and Prabhu-ji had taken it upon himself to be the school guardian, the guardian who protected, above all, the village girls. If a girl was being taken out of school when she should be studying, Prabhu-ji would generally notice and act. He could see the school gate. Little passed him by as he held his central position in the village. The teachers knew that they were under his watchful eye and in general school enrolment was not too much of a problem in this village because of him. Beyond school attendance and the accountability of the teachers, Prabhu-ji had his eagle eye on the issue of child marriage and had instituted a fine for families trying to marry off their underage girls. Vikram introduced us and before even greeting me Prabhu-ji explained: 'Over the years I have seen too many girls, girls of fourteen, even thirteen years of age dying in childbirth. These girls should be children, not mothers, and this is God's way of showing us that marriage and childbearing at such a young age is wrong. Deeply wrong. *Bahut galat.*' The minute he opened his mouth, I was mesmerized by his slow, emphatic words.

He had such a profound message and such a learned and calm tone that it didn't surprise me that he wielded the power in the village to enforce fines, to seek out parents who were trying to break what was in fact statutory law but was still broken in villages with impunity. If Prabhu-ji so much as saw someone approach a house with laddoos, a symbol of an engagement celebration, he would be hot on their heels to ensure the girl was of appropriate age, and if not, the parents were answerable to Prabhu-ji.

I had experienced this with Sarita and Prachi, and it happened again and again. I couldn't just go into a village, knock on someone's door and convince them to send their girls to school, regardless of whether I was on a bike or on foot. I couldn't just navigate a village and understand barriers or opportunities for change. I had seen this now far too many times. The problem could not be solved that way. It had to be with the *right* leaders from *within* the village. I had posed the question, 'Was it the message or the messenger?' And now I realized the answer was both. Through these early experiences, like with Sarita and Prachi, I had learnt that it had to be a local message from a local messenger, not someone like me parachuting in from Mumbai. It didn't matter how passionate we were, how 'right' we thought we were, how sensitively we thought we were communicating our messages. These messages were not ours to tell. These stories were not ours to share.

Busy with Brushes, Not Books

If we were to challenge mindsets and change norms for girls, the message had to be community-led and community-owned. So, from speaking I shifted gears to listening. We had to listen to people like Prabhu-ji—he was the natural leader we needed to find, but we had stumbled upon him by mere chance. My next big concern was whether we would really find people with his conviction in every village.

It was at about this time that Educate Girls started working in Bhinmal block in our second district of Jalore, which included a colony of around forty households with only a small anganwadi[1] by way of a facility. The village was down a dust track, coming after the paved road stopped abruptly. This was a community on the margins. Rehman was the first Educate Girls team member to enter the community and start with a cursory survey of the families. He started off by *listening*. And what he heard was that across forty homes not a single girl had ever been to school. We planned a community meeting and at every turn were pointed in the direction of a mature lady in the village, Nadia Bano. Her reputation went before her and she was known for being wise and listened to by the community. Perhaps the development theory books had got it right this time? Was she a natural leader? So we went to visit her.

'When I was eighteen, I was married to a fifty-year-old man with five children. Five children were from his previous marriage, and then we had five together. Managing the expenses for the twelve of us was difficult. My husband used to make brooms. We managed with a little income from farming.' So her story began. 'Thirty-seven years I have lived in this colony,' she continued, 'and no one here sends their girls to school. Making jhadus [brooms] is the traditional occupation of the villagers. Girls also help their families with this work. But they work. They don't go to school.' They were busy with brooms, not books.

'Nadia Dadi' or 'Grandmother Nadia' is how the children in the village referred to her. She was, at fifty-five, the oldest lady in the village, and everyone listened to her. She had a way about her that exuded confidence and calm. She was someone who you might have thought would be bound by tradition, but after spending some time with Rehman, this was a tradition Nadia Bano was prepared to try and break with. She agreed to join our team and she started with the older girls.

Nadia Bano found ten girls aged eleven to fourteen, who were busy making brooms. She personally went to the government residential school in the block and after seeing for herself that it was a place she would have been comfortable sending her own daughters, she returned to the village to work on her neighbours. Rehman and Nadia managed to enrol all the girls in the colony in the school. This effort back in 2012 was enormous and village meetings were held to discuss it. The parents took time to come around, and the tradition took time to break. But today there is no need to break anything. Rehman and Nadia Bano allayed fears, offered up practical help and slowly changed mindsets through stories. The tradition now in this village is that the girls all go to school and girls' enrolment happens automatically each year, driven by the people of the village. It had been *their* problem and now they had solved it.

Finding the Educated Girls

Our recruitment criteria firmly said 'daughters or daughters-in-law, eighteen years old and a twelfth-grade pass'. We wanted girls, but educated girls were just not there. The men who came to the meetings with their sisters or daughters started to stand up. They too had stories and they tried to explain their connection to our cause, but this was just against my intuition.

'She can't go anywhere on her own. She can't read or write so is wholly dependent on her husband, and that means that he holds the power, the control. I get so angry when I visit because she is so isolated and so alone. She is allowed to come out with me but she can't get a job. I want her to go back to school, but she feels scared to. At least I have managed to make sure that her two daughters are enrolled in school. But she can't help them with their homework.'

Sanjay was weighed down by the burden of guilt that he had an education and his sister, Gauri, didn't. He had mobility, his sister did not.

'We used to have goats,' he explained. 'I was lucky—I got to go to school, but every afternoon when I got home, only then would I take over from my sister and take the goats up the hillside. I don't think I really thought about it much at the time as it was quite normal in our village.' He went on, 'My sister, my cousin sisters, they all stayed at home.' Gauri was in the neighbouring village. She had left home at fourteen, when Sanjay was eleven. She was married and had three children of her own.

'I never want another girl to be denied what I have. Why should I be given an education but my sister denied one?

We are the same, we are no different, we should be equal. She could also be working. But she is not. She has no freedom, while I have it all.' And Sanjay has made sure that Gauri's children go to school. She has one son and two daughters, and despite the odds, they are all going to school.

'The girls in the village are like my sisters! I will fight for them all.' This was his rallying cry, as he tried to persuade us to hire *him*. But when we first met, I wasn't ready to hire him for the village volunteer role.

She Will Not Break Stones

'She will not break stones!' That was how Asif put it when he stood up in one of our community meetings.

Because breaking stones was exactly what Asif did. Day in. Day out. His dhoti may once have been white or cream, but from the sweat and dust from the stones, it was now completely brown. Asif had the same determination as Dinesh, Vibha's father, but perhaps not the words. But I could read between every one of Asif's words, and when I asked about his motivation to educate his daughter when no one else in his village did, his assertion had the same passion. 'She will not break stones' was a resolve, a value, a pride. Asif had a vision for Salma that he knew only education could fulfil.

Asif's daughter was not going to have the life that he had had, and that was why he had ensured that Salma was an outlier in her village. Salma had completed twelve years of education in a remote, rural area, where a majority of girls were either out of school or had dropped out at fifth grade.

Salma also stood up in the meeting. Her family came from a block in Rajasthan where the out-of-school girls' numbers in most villages were incredibly high. There were large numbers of girls who had never set foot in a classroom, and plenty who had dropped out at fifth grade. As we moved from village to village, we only found young men with a twelfth-pass qualification and an ability to join our team. I was in awe of Salma for her gentle confidence, but I also saw in her father something of my own. He also held a pride and an ambition for his daughter beyond the social norm. Not from a need to conform, but a comfort in being different.

We hired Salma. But first we turned Sanjay down, along with other men like him. I was adamant in the early days, and my early assumptions told me that we needed a female force to drive the message home, to build on lived experience and have women to work in the villages and enrol girls. But for every four twelfth-pass men we managed to find, who wanted to work with us, we were probably only finding one woman. The numbers exposed the reality that in deep rural India, women were not able to stay in school.

I really grappled with this. Apart from the fact that I believed we needed female volunteers, I had my aunt, Mahe, in my peripheral vision all the time. The aunt who fought for me. The aunt who got me back into school. And I believed it was an 'aunt' I needed for all these girls, not an uncle. But I also believed firmly that we needed a workforce that modelled equality—how could I lead a feminist organization that was fighting for gender equity if I had a workforce of men? And so I persisted. Until reality showed me that there was a missing generation—no matter how hard we looked, we were not going to find that army of women with a twelfth-grade pass qualification. We had to think differently.

The data was telling me that hundreds, thousands and millions of girls were out of school. I wanted to expand to the next district and the district after that, but we weren't finding enough educated girls to make this vision a reality. At the time only around 4 per cent of girls in rural India were completing higher secondary school.[2] There was a conflict here—we knew that we needed a girl in every village to work in *their* village, but we also knew that girls in rural India very, very rarely completed twelve years of education, let alone twelfth grade.[3]

Should I persist with hiring only female field staff to work with Vikram and Meena, or did I need to rethink this? I was still not convinced we could have male champions fighting for girls.

He for She

There was a lesson I needed to learn, and I learnt it when I met Kamlesh. But it took me a while.

Kamlesh's father was a public-school teacher, but he wasn't all that taken by the idea of a government job himself. Kamlesh liked to meet lots of people and travel, and he wanted to get out of the village for work. Much to the chagrin of his father, he took up work as a taxi driver. Now, there are taxi drivers and there are taxi drivers, and when I met him, I could see that Kamlesh was one of the confident, outgoing characters who would engage with his passengers and always have a story to tell or an inquiry to make. He is an imposing man with a bright twinkle in his eye. His well-groomed beard told me he took pride in his appearance and his culture. A bear-like figure that could either intimidate you or make you feel safe and protected, Kamlesh first met us when he accompanied his wife to a recruitment event.

Joining Educate Girls wasn't an obvious choice for him. But when his wife started volunteering, Kamlesh was intrigued and deeply moved by her engagement and success in enrolling girls in his village school. Over the course of a year, Kamlesh saw how every day she would meet with families, teachers and village leaders. He saw how she journeyed to the furthest hamlets of the village to seek out girls and persuade their families to send them to school, and occasionally he joined her for a particularly challenging conversation. Kamlesh, unlike his wife, was not the obvious candidate, and so our team did indeed take over a year to be convinced to give him a chance. But when they did, they saw an opportunity.

Two years on, and stones were still being thrown by Ram in the village where Vikram first got hit, and the villagers were still brewing their own liquor. It was still held back by a generation of men who couldn't find work, who took solace in alcohol, kept their girls at home and sent their wives out to earn a daily wage or sit in the neighbouring market with some meagre produce from their tiny strips of land. It was a near-impossible cluster of villages and was far from the main Highway 32 that took you up and over the Aravali Hills in the direction of Jodhpur. There was very little support from the teacher there, and the school remained half-empty. She had enough to do to try and engage the children in their classes.

The numbers had dropped in her school, funding from the government had reduced and she didn't have the money to mend the stinking toilet, nor to get the water pump pumping.

'I enrolled ten girls in my first four months.' Kamlesh told me proudly. 'I'm a taxi driver. I'm used to conversations. I can be very persuasive, and I don't take no for an answer and a drunken passenger doesn't worry me!'

Having seen his wife at work in their village and heard her stories of negotiations and tactics, he was able to deploy some of the same, mixed with his own passion and belief that every girl had the right to go to school and it was for the benefit of the whole village as well as each family. He used the fact that his father was a government teacher to build credibility and also speak from experience about how important education is. But he also used his talent with inebriated passengers to engage with Ram and others like him in the village, who struggled with alcohol addiction and had pushed themselves and their families deep into the margins.

A father-to-father chat is what often clinches the deal. Working behind the scenes in the village to get the male head master and the male Gram Panchayat[4] leadership on their side is also a tactic where a man-to-man interaction can work. The surprise in some communities of seeing a man working for the girls is enough to provoke change. Gender equality is powerful with men as part of the solution.

Quite often, the most powerful advocate is someone who has also made a profound change themselves—former smokers are often the most vociferous anti-smoking campaigners! There is nothing more powerful than a father explaining to a fellow neighbour why he was persuaded by Educate Girls to enrol his daughters in school.

And that brings me back to Ram. It was grief that had brought Ram's life to a halt. Before his wife died, he was a successful farmer and an educated man. His wife had also studied and worked. His girls had actually been to school before, but once their mother died he had pulled them out. With no income, Ram even had to resort to selling items from the house. Kamlesh remembered one time asking why they were building a fire from wood, and Pooja replied that her father had sold the gas canister to pay for liquor. But as he got to know Ram, he realized there was potential here. Pooja pleaded with her father to send her and her sisters to school. Kamlesh could see Ram was intelligent, and likely with his story a powerful influencer. Through leaning into Ram's memories of his wife, Kamlesh managed to reignite aspiration in Ram. Ram is now one of the most tenacious Team Balika we have, and he is now back to his farming. He became our gateway to the village, our ears, our eyes, our heart and our action. Kamlesh and he were the reason that most of the children in the village were now going to school. And they both were the reason that I managed to change my own mindset and challenge my biases. Having thrown stones in our path, eventually Ram joined us *on our path* and saw how powerful an education would be for his girls.

This story showed me just how much stronger we are when we work together. I went into this work with strong feminist ideals and a bias that only a woman could truly champion girls' education from her own position and lived experience. How wrong I was and how clearly I saw that in

Ram, Kamlesh, Asif, Sanjay and countless others, who have joined our team that we had passionate male advocates for girls who spoke a whole different language and told different stories to shift mindsets—as they shifted my own!

It took me a while, but I got there in the end, and we now had a really clear idea of who we were looking for to engage with communities. We thought it was just the elders, but we found people young and old who joined our team. We learnt not to judge by appearances but truly listen to the inhabitants of each and every village and we finally overcame my rigidity around working with women alone. We found a great many men, old and young, with the drive and influence to fight for girls' education.

The team was coming together. As we grew we also gathered more and more stories, honing our message and becoming more and more authentic as the story married the storyteller. We had hired Meena, Vikram, Ramlal and Vijayalakshmi, and others were joining us as our work spread from village to village. But something still wasn't quite right. A voice in my head kept asking me, 'How do we know we are finding *every* girl? How do we know that we haven't missed anyone?' And this takes me right back to the very beginning of the Educate Girls story, and how we decided where to start and how to find every last girl.

5

Lessons in How to Count Girls

'I wisely started with a map!'

—J.R.R. Tolkien

As the team came together, we realized we needed to know where to look and how to find every out-of-school girl in every village. Where should we look? At first, we thought the answer was easy. Each school had a list of out-of-school girls. And once we had a partnership with the government, they were happy to share it so we could mobilize families and bring those girls back into school. We needed a plan and a system. But something nagged at us: Did those lists share the full picture? Were we really finding every last girl?

Counting Girls

'Arre waah!' he trumpeted, waving a hand in the air to signal success and draw everyone's attention to him. In his other hand, he held a steaming hot glass of chai by its rim. This was a celebration toast.

'We have enrolled eighteen girls. Every girl on the list! Bhakti, Parvati, Laxmi, Pinki ...' He reeled off names, proud that he knew them all. Every girl on his list was important, previously out of school and now gracing his classroom every day. He was a happy man. All the girls were now going to school.

The mood was quite jubilant. Just four months ago Mr Shankar had presented us with a list of out-of-school girls in his village. He was the head teacher and had been grateful for our support. The atmosphere at the school was one of pride and satisfaction. I might even dare to say we were all a little smug! 100 per cent enrolment. We had done it. Having spent the first couple of hours of the day singing and dancing with the classes, we then sat with the girls to see how they were getting on. Some girls were still incredibly shy and found it hard to articulate what they thought about being students rather than working in the fields. For them, the change had been so enormous. But others had a newfound confidence that radiated from them as they showed us what they had learnt. They told us stories of reading to their grandmothers, often still balancing chores at home, but they were clearly happy, very happy that they were now going to school. Even Bharti, a slight little girl I had met a few months before whose parents had been very inflexible about the idea of school, had made enormous progress and showed me how she could write her name in both Devanagari and the alphabet. We patted ourselves on the back.

Leaving the school, Vikram, Meena and I scoured the village and decided upon a shaded wall beside a pond, not far from the water pump, to sit and open up our dabbas. Manju-ji from our guest house had packed a delicious lunch of roti, sabzi and achaar and we passed each individual steel pot around sharing the vegetables and dal, digging in with our fingers and relishing each mouthful. In the distance, we could hear the school bell go and the children pour out of the classrooms into the courtyard, their playful voices all merged into that sound that we all know as the 'playground' sound—a sound that cannot be mistaken for anything else—chatter and the odd delirious scream usually associated with a win, whether it be kabaddi or kho-kho, tag or cricket.

But just as we were easing into our feeling that in this village our job was done, four girls rounded the corner and approached the well. All four were barefoot, each carrying a shiny steel urn. The smallest could not have been more than six years old; the other three looked to me like they were around eight or nine. School was still in full flow, albeit it being recession. There were still another few hours in the classroom before the children went home. Why were these girls not in school?

I don't think any of us wanted to ask the question at first as we were still too focused on our celebrations, convinced we had enrolled everyone on our list, every last girl in the village. Perhaps they were just absent that day. Enrolled girls do tend to have to miss some school sometimes. So we carried on eating, but this time in silence. The unease was kicking in as we watched the girls with their sinewy arms heave on the water pump and then hoist the urns up and onto their heads. No doubt all of us were thinking the same thing. We avoided eye contact. Then another couple of girls approached the well, and then another. As we sat there, in the space of an hour while eating our lunch, over nine girls came to fill water. When the tenth little girl approached the well, we decided to speak to her.

We asked her where she lived and she gestured far across the valley behind a small temple whose tiny orange flag we could just see poking out above a clump of trees. We asked her if she went to school. 'No' was her simple answer as she shook her head, unable to look me in the eye. We asked her if she was enrolled in the school. She said no. And after a while, after sitting with her for twenty minutes or so, we learnt that there were at least twenty-one girls in her community on the periphery of the village and none of them were going to school.

What we couldn't understand was why they weren't on our all-important list, the list that Mr Shankar at the school had given us. What did we miss?

Where to Start

The revelation in Mr Shankar's village perplexed us as we hadn't just landed up in this village by chance. It wasn't just a list we had stumbled upon, we had followed a process, we had thought we had been highly strategic about our work plan, about how we were going to find girls who were out of school.

Sharing this story takes me right back to when I first returned to India and why we started in Rajasthan. I had started delving into the reports and statistics and it was clear that there was a big problem in terms of the high number of girls who were out of school. But despite the numbers, even back then, it wasn't a problem everywhere. As I mentioned before, Hans Rosling said, 'Go to the margins!'[1] but I soon realized I needed to know *which* margins to go to. Finding girls in a country the size of India—a country of over 1 billion people—felt like trying to find needles in a haystack.

A lot of people start an NGO programme in 'their' village. But I was very clear from the beginning that this was not going to be my approach. I didn't *have* a village. There was no 'my' village. I could have stuck a pin on a map and I'm sure we would have found some out-of-school girls. But I'm not a gambler. I'm a great one for knowing what I don't know, and quite obsessed with data and with process (it's perhaps the economist in me). I needed to work with the people who did know. I wanted to look at the numbers and I wanted to design a system and what I needed was a meaningful list. Surely the government would have the details of girls who weren't in school. So that was my first port of call. I decided to go and ask the government.

I found myself in the offices of the Ministry for Human Resource Development (MHRD) in Shastri Bhavan, New Delhi, a short distance from the Parliament House and India Gate. This was the decision-making powerhouse of everything schooling and education in India, and a good friend in Mumbai knew a certain minister personally and had given us a warm introduction. It was a sprawling seven-storey building, and as I peered at the signs in the downstairs lobby, I could see that it housed a curious combination of ministries including Law and Justice, Broadcasting and Petroleum—I had to make sure I found the correct elevator. And I did.

There were a few of us perched on white plastic chairs lined up against the wall of the corridor. The minister made short shrift with the trendy television executive who was trying to sell her content to be included in the national curriculum. I had wondered if she was in the wrong ministry. As she launched into a nervous rehearsed pitch, the minister, standing in his doorway, refused to even invite her into his office. Looking decidedly distracted, he said a firm 'No!' before she really got started. Another sales manager of an education company received a similar response—the minister waved him away, 'You are far too expensive!' he huffed, and the salesman stumbled off down the corridor, typing frantically into his Blackberry.

And then there was me. I didn't hold out much hope, having witnessed these two brusque dismissals. I stood in the way of the minister and his lunch. Yet, his eyes met with mine and warmed to a certain degree, I thought. Perhaps I was less out of place in my soft pink salwar kameez rather than the sharp suits of the previous two candidates.

'I have a meeting I am already late for. I literally have five minutes,' he announced.

'Sir,' I responded, 'I really only need five.'

And then he listened and nodded, and I genuinely think he heard me. I told him about our girls, I told him about what I was reading in my research and what I was seeing as I travelled across the country. There were enormous numbers of girls in rural India who were not going to school. I then asked him to help us build a programme for scale. I needed access to schools and a government-endorsed plan to take our approach across forty districts in India, and most importantly I needed to know where to start.

'We can help.' He agreed far quicker than I had imagined even although I had run over my five minutes. But my ask was simple, my pitch was tight. The two ladies who were assisting him turned to me once he had left the room. They then handed over a list, that all-important list I was looking for. But it wasn't a list of out-of-school girls. Instead, it was a list of 'critical gender gap districts' that pointed to Rajasthan as an epicentre with nine out of the twenty-six worst districts in the entire country.

'Of course education is a state matter, Ms Husain, you understand, you will have to go to Rajasthan to take approval there, but the minister's recommendation will go far!' one of the ladies insisted in a curt but encouraging tone.

And so it began. We had a plan.

Going Where the Gender Gap Gapes

Based on research at the time, we estimated that there were well over 7 million[2] primary-aged girls who were missing from India's classrooms and who should have been in school. If we wanted to make sure we weren't going to lose another generation of girls to poverty and illiteracy, we had to act fast and identify where the problem was greatest—where did a majority of the out-of-school girls live? I wanted to use the government's gender gap list to help me decipher where to start.

The World Economic Forum first published an annual report that looked at the gender gap in 2006[3] and studied four dimensions: economics, education, health and politics. It's perhaps no coincidence then that when I first started looking for data, this is what we were talking about. And the 'gender gap' in education was quite simply the gap in enrolment numbers between girls and boys in primary school. Essentially, in many areas, there was a 10–20 per cent gap between the number of girls and the number of boys going to school. And of course the number of girls going to school was a lot lower than the number of boys.

In 2007, India was divided into around 600 districts and twenty-six had what was described as the 'worst gender gap in education'. Of those, a majority of nine districts were all in Rajasthan. So there I had my first piece of the puzzle. This was where I had to start. I had, with one list, managed to narrow down the problem from everywhere across the country to one state, and from a haystack of 600 districts to what I believed were the nine worst districts in the country. I might not have found our needle yet, but I'd already cleared out a lot of the hay!

Heeding the MHRD minister's advice, I went to meet the Rajasthan state education minister in Jaipur, and together we decided to officially start in the district of Pali, one of the worst of the nine. These nine districts on the government's list formed a 'V' shape if you plotted them on a map, and at the centre and lowest point sat Pali, somewhat like a pendant hanging on a necklace. If I started in Pali, a kind of hotspot or epicentre, I could then move in both directions, north-east and north-west, and cover the next eight districts with ease. This was my thinking.

Administrative districts in India are further divided into 'blocks' before you then get down to the village Gram Panchayat level. So, within Pali, the education minister allocated three of these areas, deemed as 'development blocks', in which to start work, work that had his valuable approval. These were areas where rain-fed agriculture was the major source of income, but as a drought-prone area, infertile soil and a shortage of water forced large numbers of people to migrate all the way to Madhya Pradesh or Gujarat for six to eight months every year. This focus area also had a population overwhelmingly from what was first described in 1980 as OBC, the population that still makes up 40–45 per cent of India's 1.4 billion people.[4] When I first went to Pali, the government told me that a mere 44 per cent of women in the district were able to read.[5] And in my mind's eye, I could immediately see the other 56 per cent. As I write this now, I can see Jassi's mum, who nearly lost her savings to the bank she thought she could trust, and Poonam, who lost her land to a scheming nephew, all because she couldn't read. This plan was for them.

I had in just a few pivotal meetings confirmed that Rajasthan was the *right* state in which to expand this work, the state with a majority of the country's most gender-unequal districts. It might seem unbelievable, but this is how government meetings go sometimes. Meeting the right person at the right time with the right introduction can work magic. I had been given enormous insight into the districts in which we should start our work, and then the government data even showed me the right blocks in which to start outreach! This was about as strategic as it got and, most importantly, it was a plan backed by the government!

But as the gaps in Mr Shankar's list showed us, neither a list of out-of-school girls nor a list of gender gap districts was going to be all we needed.

Let the Count Begin

We were in a white Mahindra Commander jeep, and beginning to wonder if it had any functioning suspension at all. Conversation was erratic, and our knuckles were white. Twelve of us were crowded into the open-top vehicle, and two by two we dropped off the teams at the edge of each village where they were to start their school information campaign. Having left the tar road, we were now bumping along a pitted and dusty track, baked hard in the sun. Rajasthan was eight months away from the last rains, and it was still perhaps a month before the monsoon would break, so the track was sparing no one, the land was hard and thirsty.

Despite growing up in Delhi, India's most populous city, and the second-largest city in the world by population, I'm really a rural girl at heart, by necessity rather than privilege. As a full-time working mum, my mother was unable to care for me when the school doors were shut. Her village friends and relatives were far more likely to be able to accommodate me than neighbours in the city. So I was packed off most holidays. But never was I happier than in these far-flung places, Pilibhit or Clutterbuck Ganj near Bareilly in Uttar Pradesh or Ramnagar near Corbett National Park. So many summers and monsoons were spent in those places.

Simple village life had shaped my difficult childhood, despite the fact that I was essentially a city-dweller, and I was excited to be going back now, on a mission.

As you enter any village in India, you are likely to see a school building quite soon. This village was no different, and we pulled up to the low boundary wall. Peering over, we could see the children, straight-backed and seated in rows on striped rugs laid out on a polished veranda that ran the length of the building, a couple of steep steps above the dusty playground, almost like a stage. Others spilled out from the classroom, making the most of the natural light, rather than relying on the small bare light bulbs that dangled and swayed with the breath from the fan that nonchalantly moved the hot air around. Today, the fan fanned and the light was lit. But on other days when there was a power cut, the classrooms were airless and dark.

I popped my head around the door and children's eyes stared up at me. Some eyes were apprehensive, others cheeky and curious. The headteacher took me aside after the class and we sat on two white plastic chairs at one end of the veranda, chairs that were these days as common in offices in Delhi as they were in the most remote village. One of the children's mothers, who cooked the midday meal approached carrying a steel tray with the anticipated yet welcome cup of chai.

We had come to this village to start building our village profile. The principal secretary of education had allocated fifty schools in these three development blocks, and this was where we were starting our very first programme (twenty-five in Pali and twenty-five in the neighbouring Jalore district). The job at hand now was to understand the current status of the schools, and of the girls. We were going to record details about the school size, teachers, availability of learning materials and midday meals. We would list the state of the infrastructure: Did it have electricity, running water or a playground, was there a functioning toilet and a separate one for girls? How were the children's grades?

But most importantly, we were going to look at the enrolment numbers, and as we sat there with the head teacher, the first thing she did was hand us a list before we had even asked. This felt easy! She opened up a slightly scruffy-looking A4 exercise book with a marbled cover and pale green lined pages, and as she ran her finger down the page, she explained that to the best of her knowledge, this list accounted for the girls in the village who had either dropped out or never been enrolled.

These were the lists that we used for the first year or so as we slowly made our way around the first few blocks in Pali and Jalore. We had lists, we found girls, we enrolled girls—we certainly thought the system was working.

Asking the Right Questions

This approach was followed for two whole enrolment seasons, two whole years of work. From the end of the school exams in March through to July each year, we went to the allocated schools, met the head teachers and took their list of girls. But we were starting to see a pattern emerge.

One afternoon, I was tempted to ask for another cup of chai, but it was already eleven and we hadn't even really started what we had come to do. If we carried on much past noon the May sun would start to dry the sweat and burn the skin. As we started to make our way around the village, on just an initial glance up the winding road that dissects the village, I could see a number of girls crouched on their doorsteps, their dupattas wrapped around them, their ghagras hitched up to stop them from getting in the way of their work, washing lentils or chopping onions.

We continued around the village, following the list, chatting with parents and gathering a small following of characters from the village who seemed keen to help. We had pretty much exhausted the list and met the parents of most of the girls recorded, but it seemed there might be more.

'You might find some other girls down by the water,' one of the taggers-along mentioned, pointing across the field that fell down to a slight trickle of water—an apology for a stream. Even the stream was thirsty for the monsoon. Five more girls were indeed across the field, scrubbing clothes, and another couple were at the water pump, filling steel vessels that blinded us as they reflected the baking sun at the peak of its elevation. They were not on the list, but were visible if you looked hard enough. We started to realize that there were a lot of girls who were not on our lists for one reason or another. We needed to understand why—who were these girls and what made them invisible?

Our first realization was that if a girl lived outside the school catchment, she wouldn't be on the list. Girls in the hamlets outside of the catchment didn't count. It appeared that the lists of out-of-school girls were following a system, following rules rather than following the girls. There were clear boundaries demarcated by the local government, and catchment areas that did not in any way flex to incorporate any additional girls. The houses across the valley, the areas that fell between villages, those on the margins, that I have described to you before, often fell between school catchments. It was like a kind of no man's land. We were back to those physical margins again. 'If you live near the crossroads, you're going to be okay. But if you live on the margins, the world is going to forget about you.' I can hear Hans Rosling again, and we were seeing this with our own eyes.

We then started to realize that there were girls, no matter where they lived, who were also not on the list as they simply did not exist in the eyes of the authorities. In 2005, only 40 per cent of childbirths in India took place in a health facility, and in rural communities only 28 per cent of children were not delivered at home.[6] Parents' education and wealth is a strong determining factor in whether or not they give birth at home or in a medical institution. If you are poor, and have not had the benefit of education, you are far more likely to have your baby without the help of a medical practitioner. Many of the girls we met were born at home, and this is not necessarily always a problem, except it is a leading cause of high maternal mortality and can lead to births not being recorded. Without a birth certificate, girls can easily 'disappear'. Time and time again we met families who had not been approached by the school or the district education officer (DEOs) as their girls truly were invisible to the system. Their births had never been recorded, so how would the authorities know they existed? How could they ever be counted?

And then there were the bahuen, the daughters-in-law, the child brides. When we came to Aarti's house we learnt another important lesson. Aarti was seven years old, and we had enrolled her back in April 2009. We returned in June that same year to check if she was all ready for school as the start of the school year was just around the corner. Aarti's parents had taken a bit of convincing, but her two older brothers had completed their tenth and so they did believe in education. Aarti used to help a lot around the house so that her mother could work. But with no younger siblings, in the end Aarti's mother decided she could now go to school and the housework would still get done somehow.

On our second visit, however, we noticed another girl in the back room of their home. She didn't look up when we entered and was not introduced to us by Aarti's parents. This little girl was veiled. She must have been about twelve or thirteen, and was busy rolling out dough into round chapatis on a small wooden plinth by the fire. We glanced down again at our list of girls, a little confused, but the list clearly said that Aarti was the only girl in the house. We felt a little awkward, but eventually enquired as to who was making the meal in the next room.

'That's Sheetal, our daughter-in-law,' Aarti's mother explained in a nonchalant tone.

On our first visit to Aarti's house back in April, we had asked about the family, following our usual questionnaire. The sons were over eighteen so we hadn't dwelled on them. We learnt that Aarti's father, Jagdish, was a labourer with a local construction firm, and Aarti's mother, Meenu, worked through the MGNREGA. We had asked about the children in the house and Meenu had mentioned all three of *her* children. And then of course Aarti became our focus as she was at the time not going to school and had missed the reception year. We had gotten our answers, we made our enrolment plan, but had we asked the *right* questions?

What we hadn't asked was—are there any *other* girls in the house? We hadn't enquired if Meenu and Jagdish's sons were married. A daughter-in-law, a bahu, was not part of our enquiry. Sheetal was invisible. Out of school, not on anyone's list. And this was not a rare occurrence. In 2024, India still accounted for one in three of the world's child brides. An estimated 1.5 million girls got married each year before the age of eighteen, and given that the Prohibition of Child Marriage Act only came into law in 2006, when we first started work we came across this situation many, many times—58 per cent of young women in Rajasthan aged between eighteen and twenty-nine years said they had married before they were eighteen when interviewed by the National Family Health Survey in 2005–06.[7] Being a bride meant in so many eyes that you were no longer a child, you no longer counted as a 'girl'.

When the Lists Don't Work

In this very first pilot programme, we found 885 girls who had either never been enrolled in school or had been forced to drop out: 885 girls on the margins, invisible to the authorities, some born at home, some brides, no longer children—all missing from lists. This was twice the number provided by the schools. In most villages, we were finding close to double the amount of girls mentioned in the school's list. The numbers all had names. We had exercise books with names and numbers, we then had Excel spreadsheets that eased the quantification back in the office, when Vikram managed to get to our one and only computer. But every number was a girl, every girl had a story, and every girl had to go to school.

After two years, we managed to enrol just over half the out-of-school girls in our two pilot blocks. Then just two years later, after our 500-school pilot, we had honed our programme and the out-of-school girls figure reduced to a mere 1 per cent of the female school-going population. Only one in 100 girls in our districts in 2009 was now not going to school.[8] This was deemed a great success. But I didn't feel that success. The voice inside me was a worried voice. 'This isn't enough; what if I haven't done a good enough job?'

That 1 per cent was still 279 little girls. This was a recurring niggling feeling whenever I reviewed our lists. The marks on the page would start to swim in front of my eyes, and whenever I saw a name, I saw a face. The numbers stayed on the page, but the girls entered my head. I saw Vibha on the back of her brother's bike. I saw Sheetal, in a dark corner of her in-laws' hut, slaving over a hot stove, her husky voice telling a story of dangerous smoke fumes without the need for words. And I saw myself in some of my darkest days when I too was out of school. And there was my hypervigilance rearing its face.

'What if there are more? What if there are more girls? What if we miss one girl?' It seemed quite clear to us all that this wasn't a robust enough system; the lists weren't foolproof.

A Census for Girls

By 2010, with a few years' experience and a deeper understanding of the missing data, I decided to suggest a dramatically different approach. Rather than working backwards from the schools' lists of out-of-school girls, I felt we had no choice but to take on a full village survey ourselves—a comprehensive census for girls!

'Are you mad?' the team exclaimed. 'You want to knock on every door?'

As recommended by the UN, all countries must conduct a decennial survey. To date in India, the government has knocked on every door of its vast population sixteen times. The very first census was published in 1872, and the 2021 census, delayed because of COVID, is still much awaited. But it is a huge endeavour, requiring enormous manpower and massive costs. The team thought that this was a crazy suggestion, an impossible task.

'We are not the government!' they announced, hoping to draw a line under the idea.

But I genuinely felt we had no choice. By 2010, the 2001–02 census was becoming very outdated. The schools' data was inaccurate. During the 500-school programme we had to deliver detailed reports to the government as part of our agreement to work alongside the public schools. So, in order to demonstrate the need for a better list of out-of-school children, we undertook a full door-to-door survey in four villages, giving us the ability to compare the government list with ours. There was resistance and criticism at first, but once the government spot-checked our data through a significant village-level sample audit, they agreed—

our figures were 98 per cent accurate. Our out-of-school girl numbers were a lot more accurate than theirs, and depressingly, a lot bigger. The picture we were painting was dismal, but the need for our own new census for girls was clearly established. Importantly, the government agreed, and our Educate Girls team, although daunted by the plan, also eventually backed me up.

Mapping Their World

Eighty per cent of Indian addresses are written with respect to a landmark which typically lies between 50 and 1,500 metres from the actual location of the home. And the area covered by a pin code can be anything from 1.5 and 179 square kilometres,[9] an area that could conceivably hold close to a hundred thousand households! This wasn't going to be an easy job, but I was tenacious, and luckily for me the team was too.

'First we have to map the village,' Vikram explained, quietly but firmly. If we were going to do this, we had to do it properly, systematically!

As I threw about wild ideas of a census, Vikram was the member of the team who took the lead and channelled my vision and honed it into what was to become our all-important village entry strategy that is today still guiding us as we enter entirely new states, not just new districts. Without a robust address system, we needed to create our own, and for that we needed a village meeting.

The East India Company's Survey of India produced the very first professional map of the country, published finally in 1779 after around thirteen years of work, and today we have Survey of India (SoI) maps and of course Google. But we needed a very different type of map, nothing historical, nothing so slow—we needed a 'real-time' map. We called a group of elders in this first village, who sat for a day with a huge piece of chart paper and coloured pens.

The way we began was by agreeing upon the margins of the village—not an easy feat, but we needed to identify the furthest first. The map was of course not to scale, but once the boundary was set, we worked inwards with deep discussion and contributions from everyone identifying every important 'chota mota' (little) landmark and every home and numbering them. We ignored the government's school catchment.

'Anilbhai's house is over there by the temple,' one of the team members offered up.

'Yes, and there are at least three other homes that side,' one of the older men agreed.

'And do we know if there are any girls there?' we enquired.

No one was sure, but we would go and find out. The chart paper was a web of lanes, numbers and Devanagari script by the time we finished it, and the job the next day was to start at home number one, and then go and knock on every single door.

Going the Last Mile

This was our very first door-to-door survey—something that is now the backbone of our organization. That day, when we conducted our questionnaire for the first time, I was sure there was no way I thought in my wildest dreams that we would top 14 million household visits nearly two decades later.

The questionnaire had been designed by Vikram. We had very different styles, Vikram and I, and he was perhaps a little surprised that I insisted on testing the survey myself. He had thought deeply about each question in the tool and it was our job that day to test how well the questions worked with the village interviewees and the breadth of team members engaged in the asking. Vikram's assumption was that we should follow the map and diligently go from house to house. And he was right. But knowing that he would follow the system, I had a far more reactive approach and found myself almost immediately attracting a crowd.

'*Bahar se aaye hain*! [They are outsiders],' the cry went out, and I was immediately surrounded.

'*Mumbai se hai*?' was the first question—or was it actually a statement, a knowing declaration that didn't really require an answer. You are from Mumbai.

Was it my accent? My dress? Whatever it was, it attracted attention. Vikram, on the other hand, looked and sounded 'right'. He combined the traditional with the new in his tan curled-toe jutti (slippers), his denim jeans and an immaculately pressed pistachio kurta. He was the local; he was our licence to operate.

As we started to move around the village, from house to house, what started as one or two children following me, barefooted and curious, turned into quite a crowd, with a handful of youth from the village offering their support, causing what Vikram could only describe as 'drama and a distraction'. He was not amused. 'I could do this in half the time if I was on my own,' he declared, but secretly I think he was moved by the children's engagement in our mission.

Vikram was wise. He still is. We were contemporaries, but I always deferred to him, given his deep understanding of Pali. He was born and raised there, and if anyone could design effective strategies to challenge persistent, discriminatory social norms, it was Vikram, because he understood context, he had lived and breathed these villages and communities his whole life.

'There are no children in that house, Didi,' the children cried. They knew everything!

'Here they don't go to school, here they are bahut gareeb [too poor], and their children never come to school.' A matter-of-fact statement.

The children confidently assessed the village, door to door, street to street, and shared their expert knowledge. This was the intelligence we needed, being crowdsourced by a group of hopping and skipping youngsters, and some of the other older ones applied later on to work with us. But Vikram was right—We still needed to complete the survey and follow the meticulously designed system. We couldn't miss anyone. I was a distraction, but I was loving it! And what we ended up doing worked. While Vikram worked with the tools and the process, I was building relationships and trust, listening and seeking out our natural leaders. This was the winning combination for effective community mobilization. We had to have the perfect balance between data collection and relationship collection! The door-to-door survey gave us both.

But counting girls wasn't as straightforward as just following a map. Not only did we have to go to the extreme margins of the villages, ask the right questions about daughters and daughters-in-law and navigate the complexity of birth certification and age proof, we also had to work with things like joint families. Knocking on one door did not necessarily mean we would find one family. Within the confines of a boundary wall we might find multiple family units living together, but often very much socially apart. One family would only answer for their nuclear family, and we missed many girls by not speaking with every family member. In a joint family, very often each mother had her own cooking pots and fire. We improved our system by counting not just a home, but each stove and mother, and we linked our count to every stove in the household, not just the actual physical home. So our intricate numbering system that we painted on the walls included a count for every mother in the home. We were determined to leave nothing to chance.

Over the River

The system was like a machine!

'We have an average run rate of about forty houses a day,' Vikram explained in a very businesslike manner, or perhaps that was my terminology he was repeating back to me, as I had flashbacks from my economics degree days. We were a few months on, and Vikram was talking with deep experience of a successful household survey that we were now rolling out at the beginning of the next school year as we expanded our outreach to new districts. When the girls were in school or there were no children in the household, the door-to-door survey was pretty quick—we could indeed cover around forty houses in a day. On other days it might take half a day to reach just one home.

Today was one of those days. While I had been to one village and surveyed around thirty houses, Sanjay and Swati had crossed a river to find just one. They looked exhausted. 'There was one last house and—we thought—one last girl. We hadn't been there yet,' Sanjay had announced at lunchtime. The map had been created in a highly consultative manner, and Sanjay, with the help of the Panchayat Raj and a couple of other village members, had worked hard to ensure that we covered the full village—every hamlet across the fields that only just counted as the village.

Sanjay, who we had not hired at first, was now one of our most tenacious colleagues. He was a short but robust young man of twenty-two, who had grown up in the terrain, a terrain that tested your physicality and obviously shaped your form. He was strong and had a face that shared wisdom and resilience beyond his years.

And this was a very hilly village. In any normal school, a more urban school perhaps, Sanjay would likely be an athlete, but his fitness was born of work, his strength came from the geography. Today he almost looked like an athlete, sporting a crimson collared polo shirt.

We were having our end-of-day debrief, and Sanjay insisted on taking us down to the edge of the river. I was exhausted, but his enthusiasm was infectious. He had a story to tell. So we followed him out past what was the last house we had surveyed and down the side of the hill, behind which the sun was starting to hide itself.

'There,' he pointed, 'that's the house!'

There was a vast body of water that stood between us and what Sanjay insisted was a dwelling. My eyes were starting to fail me and I had to take his word for it. The river was really about a kilometre from where you would assume the village ended, but no, it continued across the river and up the opposite bank. As our mapping process insisted, every family had to be part of some village. Everyone needed to belong. But this was far. If I really squinted, I could just about make out a tiny cluster of huts, halfway up what was the dusty, dry hillside that rose out of the water and would be transformed and green when the monsoons came. As too would the river.

It looked wider than a river—it was more like a lake. But scanning left and then right there was no end to it, so it must be flowing to and from somewhere. The surface was a khaki green, the colour of a military uniform, and it appeared like the water halted at a very steep, ashen rockface, rather than an accessible bank. I could not even imagine how they had crossed the river, let alone landed on the other side. At that moment as we took it all in, it was quite still, like a mirror, and the reflection of the hillside, inverted, stretched back towards us.

'Once the rains come,' Sanjay said in a warning tone, 'the river gains a new life. Currently, it stands still. Any time soon it will lap up the monsoon and start to really flow.'

Sanjay continued with his day's story. There wasn't a boat, but a local farmer who also had a tiny strip of land on the other side of the river, where he grew gourds, had agreed to ferry them across. He had tied three large bamboo logs together, and instead of a paddle he used a stick with a plastic lid attached to it with twine.

'We were obviously going to get wet, but we had to go,' he recalled.

The farmer usually traversed the water alone, so it was a push for the three of them to board his raft, and at one point Sanjay and Swati took off their shoes and used them to paddle furiously to try and halt what felt like a slow submersion. But there was a steely determination to leave no girl behind. They reached, but then had the hillside to scale before they could complete the task, ask the questions and add Pinki to their list.

'Pinki had never been to school,' Sanjay continued, not sounding surprised, but his voice was full of empathy, and some personal pride.

Writing on the Wall

As they departed, Sanjay left our signature on the wall of Pinki's home, our Educate Girls logo and a unique number, whose meaning was known only to us. Odd, you might think, but let me explain. My vigilance extended to my obsession with data verification and attribution, and we had insisted on a system where we could send in auditors to cross-verify our survey, ensuring that our data was correct and that our teams were following the right process. To enable this to happen we painted our beautiful logo with sweeping blue strokes at the entrance to every house. Our logo—'she' (I like to say she!)—was a simple line drawing of a little girl's head with two pigtails and two little bows. The logo was smartly designed as the girl was made by drawing 'e' and 'g' which stood for our organization's name. It was such a win to have a simple logo. It helped us become part of the community. The logo was also highly democratic. People could draw it easily. They felt it was theirs. It did not feel alien. We had no institutional language—we were plain and simple: Educate Girls.

Given the lack of an address system, we created our own, and each household was given a unique number, recorded on our map and in our list. A little girl, and a number to help everyone know that we had been there and we had counted. That way, when we returned to either cross-check or work on our enrolment campaign, we knew where to look. And what better way to instil the importance of our girls than by having a little girl's symbol adorn every household, no matter whether they had a girl or not. This was an Educate Girls village, an Educate Girls hamlet, and a community that was slowly beginning to believe in its girls. And even today, as you drive through the districts where we have worked, you will be able to work out the Educate Girls villages from the wall paintings.

Sanjay's narration of his afternoon was truly inspiring, and it really hit home to me that we were finding young people who fully embraced our mission of finding the very, very last girl and were dedicated to following such a thorough and rigorous process. In the time Vikram and I had covered thirty homes, Sanjay and Swati had 'only' found Pinki, but that was still a triumph. There was still work to do to persuade her family to take her to school, but they had found another precious little girl. Pinki—she had a name, she was no longer a potential or a house number on a list. She was a little girl we now knew. My mouth stretched into a wide smile of praise and celebration as I caught Sanjay's seeking eye. He had every right to be proud of such effort and tenacity, and this is what we sought time and time again.

In our first five years, we learnt a huge amount and grew our work significantly across our first two districts of Pali and Jalore. By 2012, we were working in around 4,000 schools and conducting a huge enrolment campaign on an annual basis, thousands of village meetings, doorstep conversations and hours in the classrooms. We now had a model that we knew worked; we had a rigorous system and processes for finding and recording out-of-school girls; we had an incredible team of local volunteers with deep community knowledge and engagement; and an authentic way of connecting through personal stories and stories of change, through empathy and experience, and all this shared in order to change the mindsets of families who had previously been rigid and inflexible in their attitudes and behaviour towards their girls.

PART III

Every Last Girl

6

The Making of a Movement

'The reasonable man adapts himself to the world; the unreasonable man persists in trying to adapt the world to himself. Therefore, all progress depends on the unreasonable man.'

—George Bernard Shaw,
The Power of Unreasonable People

Why are scale and saturation non-negotiables when working for gender equality? Why do we have to work at the scale of the problem when we are talking about women and girls' equality? I realized at a very early stage of my work that gender was a mindset issue that could not be tackled by talking to one person in Mumbai and one person in New Delhi, one person in New York and one in LA. Norm change happens only when a majority change their behaviour. It only happens when we have shifted the conversation from '*we* don't send our daughters to schools' to 'only *you* do not send your daughter to school'. A tipping point has to be reached. Moving girls' enrolment from the outlier to the norm has to happen everywhere, all at once. So for us, taking our work to a massive scale was imperative as this was about **every** last girl. We could not leave anyone behind.

Our strategy was now really coming together. After five years in Pali, we were ready to go further. We knew clearly *what* we had to change—namely, mindsets. We had the stories and communication strategies to make that change. We knew exactly *who* should drive this change—our local, natural leaders; one from every village. And we knew *how* and *where* to find the invisible girls and ensure that we did not miss a single one through our comprehensive door-to-door survey. We had the what, who, how and where. Our Pali and Jalore pilot projects had gone from fifty to 500 to 2,342 and then 4,000 schools by 2012.

Our first five years had been ones of looking, listening and learning, and despite setbacks and mistakes, experiments and experience led us to a place where we knew that what we were doing was slowly starting to work. The 'slowly' was the bit that worried me, however. I was in a hurry. I couldn't accept that it might take multiple generations to really close the gap for girls. This was not acceptable to me. I wanted to rapidly expand our work, not village by village, but district by district, and at a much faster rate than we had achieved in the five years since 2007. I had hired seventy people to work with me, but this model was going to be too costly, too slow, and I was in a hurry.

My urgency came from a deep personal understanding of what it was like to grow up as a girl in poverty in India, the infinite gratitude that I held and still hold for my education, and my knowledge of the size and cost of this problem. It just seemed unconscionable that we could continue to deny those who hold up half the sky their basic human rights, their right to education and to equity. These girls were the most valuable assets the world had and yet they were seen by so many as a liability.

With my economist hat on, I delved into more and more reports that quantified the problem. In 2008, it was concluded that 'India alone misses out on potential economic growth worth about $33 billion per annum, by not educating girls to the same standard as boys'.[1] This number was just unfathomable to me. This was the cost to the country. But what was the cost to each and every girl?

The consequences of inaction go beyond the global economy and are to me far, far graver. I am taken right back to Dinesh and his conclusion that without an education a girl will be treated like an animal. If a girl drops out of school she will be more likely to be a child bride. If she marries early she is more likely to have children early and be at higher risk of dying in childbirth. More vulnerable to domestic abuse, sexual abuse and trafficking. She will be less likely to immunize her children and, then, without an education, her daughter is more likely to tread a similar path of exclusion from school. This was a vicious cycle I just had to break, and fast. Annual Gender Gap Reports[2] regularly suggested that it was going to take up to 134 years to bridge this gap—and we were actually going backwards.

We had to stop another generation of girls falling into this trap. We needed to turbo-charge this approach through a large-scale and rapid gender revolution! The question was how.

Prepared to Be Unreasonable

'All my neighbours would say, "Look at this girl—she is riding a bike, her father is spoiling her, she is going to elope with someone!" I didn't listen to anyone and ignored them all!' Anisha Kumari said. She was prepared to be what her village believed was 'unreasonable'.

I met the nineteen-year-old bright, young girl with deep-set eyes and a mane of dark hair she liked to wear loose over her shoulders on a visit to a very remote part of Pali district. She too was fixated on animal analogies like me. She sat me down and regaled me with one of Premchand's classic short stories: about the oxen Hira and Moti, who had a caring master who sadly fell on hard times and sold them to a farmer who kept all his animals locked up. Until one day, when he fell asleep, Hira and Moti knocked down the shed door and helped all the animals escape. I could see where this was going!

'Girls too are imprisoned like animals!' Anisha announced with a slight desperation in her voice. 'I need to be like Hira and Moti and help them get out! Girls need to be told that this isn't all life has to offer.' And as she said this she glanced around her modest home, bereft of both furniture and light. 'Look beyond this—the world is a lot bigger than we think.' In her voice, I could hear that Anisha had the same sense of urgency as me.

In Anisha, we had found such a talented and creative advocate: a storyteller, a role model. But she hadn't been easy to find. We had travelled all night by train from Mumbai to Falna, hung out in the office for a few meetings that morning and then driven close to four hours across the district of Pali on the highway, and a further forty-five minutes practically off-road down a track that disappeared every few hundred metres and left you wondering if you were really going to arrive anywhere at all. Goats nonchalantly crossed our path. Either side of us, arid fields stretched as far as the eye could see, and the road ahead and behind was framed by bushes that leant over the road to form a kind of tunnel.

Anisha lived in a far-flung village a long way from the crossroads, deep in the interiors. Our team had been visiting her village for a couple of months before they met her. If she wasn't in the fields working, she was at home with her head in her books, studying for her BA which she was doing part-time through distance learning. To a certain extent, Anisha was invisible, but in one of our meetings with the head mistress in her village school she had proudly told us about Anisha's achievements. Anisha had passed her twelfth, she offered up with a slightly self-congratulatory tone (when really her education had very little to do with this head mistress). But we heeded her advice and went to meet Anisha.

It was almost like she had been waiting for an opportunity like Educate Girls to come along and help her channel her strong desire to fight for girls' education, I thought to myself. Anisha put all her own opportunities down to the fact that her father was an outlier, an ally and an advocate. Despite being a traditional smallhold farmer, who worked hard to provide for his family, he also did the very best he could to support his daughter. When we met him, he didn't seem like someone to challenge village norms. He wore two hooped earrings and a large white turban and was dressed in a white dhoti. But as Anisha explained, her father gave her courage and supported her to pursue her studies. He stood up for her, and she now wanted to do the same for other girls. Joining Educate Girls was going to give Anisha a focus for her mission and perhaps a sense of being part of something bigger.

'*Aage badh!* He told me to keep moving forward. He was always praising me. "My daughter is the best student," he would say, with a tear in his eye. "All I want is for you to move ahead in life."' When she was sixteen, Anisha learnt to ride a motorcycle. She was in a hurry!

'That too because of my father! Earlier I would have to walk very far with a heavy school bag to reach my secondary school. Now on my bike, I feel free of the burden. *Aasman mein udata panchi*, like a bird flying in the sky!' Again, this certainly made Anisha quite an outlier, and I could hear in her words what a persuasive and passionate champion she was going to be for the rest of the girls in her village.

I stayed on longer than the team, who had a few additional villages to visit. So, once we had finished talking, Anisha gave me a lift on her bike to the main road, where Vikram was waiting in the car for our long drive back to Falna. It was rare to see girls riding motorbikes. But she did, with her head held high, and over time her reputation in the village would change, and her 'disruption', her bike-riding and her voice for girls was no longer seen as a problem but a positive thing, with girls slowly enrolling in school and the village starting to believe in Anisha's and our mission. As I hopped into the car, I was filled with a huge sense of potential, but also a niggling fear. Despite our conviction that a great many people like Anisha exist, with such a clear and tenacious purpose and mission, the need for such an advocate in every village was so great that it seemed like an impossible task if we had to go to such lengths and rely on chance meetings and head mistress's advice to stumble upon people like Anisha. To find Anisha Kumari we had travelled miles and it had taken months.

Hope and despair clashed in my head as I struggled to really understand how on earth we were going to find an Anisha in every village, and fast! Our small core team couldn't drive down every dusty track, traverse every hill and cross every river, and then spend months in each village navigating relationships, building networks and finding these outliers one at a time. Something had to change, if we really were going to stop yet another generation of girls falling into the trap of illiteracy, if we were to somehow narrow that gender gap quickly.

A Campaign

At this time reports were telling us that 23 per cent of the world's out-of-school children were in India and of those 7 million were girls.[3] This was an enormous problem. It was 2011, and we were still only working in two districts in one state of India. And yet, the lists we were compiling of girls were getting longer and longer, and certainly reflected those grim statistics. A turning point came when the government, believing in our numbers, approached us to expand to every school in Pali district. We were of course flattered that they trusted in us and wanted us to expand so fast, but this was suddenly 2,342 schools across 1,000 villages and I knew our model would only work if we found an Anisha Kumari in every single village. How on earth was I going to find over 1,000 volunteers in time to deliver such a commitment to the government? We had to think fast and big.

'How about an event?' someone in the team suggested. I paused and reflected—this was indeed a very good idea. Even in the most remote villages people knew how to put on pretty large-scale gatherings. Usually for some kind of celebration—like a wedding or a festival. Catering, loudspeakers, a marquee—that was all very doable. This was an approach we were convinced might work. A recruitment event. We had run plenty of large block meetings before, but we still weren't sure how we would get the right people there.

'What we are going to need is a huge advertising campaign!' I announced, anticipating some eyes to roll at my 'Bombay-style' solution. I lived in Mumbai, a city that never sleeps, a city with glossy ads on every billboard and every square inch of wall, not to mention the televisions that were constantly blaring. 'But a campaign that people like Nadia Bano and Anisha Kumari will see,' I clarified. I laid down a challenge that the team immediately rose to—with a little less eye-rolling than I expected!

We had gathered in the Falna office and put our heads together to try and work out how we were going to recruit 1,000 volunteers for this exciting phase of growth. After getting on for five years of work, we knew that these natural leaders existed across Rajasthan's villages. We had met Prabhu-ji, the village priest, who policed the school gate and tackled families trying to marry off their girls too young. We had recruited Nadia Bano, the inspiring grandmother who had changed the norms in her community of broom-makers and ensured that girls now always went to school in her village instead of working. And over time, we had also found incredible allies in men like Kamlesh, Ram and Sanjay. We had met all these gender champions one village at a time, but with our expanded government partnership, we had to move from thinking village by village to thinking at a district level.

The idea of a big event was promising, but what might an advertising campaign look like if it were to reach the most remote village and inspire the interest of someone like Anisha Kumari to come along and join us? Anisha didn't have a mobile phone. Very few people did back in 2011. Between 2008 and 2020 mobile phone ownership tripled across the country, but in rural India in 2009, penetration was around 13 per cent,[4] and those phones too were mostly in the hands of men. Television wasn't really an option—the costs of a TV ad were prohibitive. We had to think long and hard about a new way of working, reaching out to people en masse.

We needed to make this really different and, from the outset, engage people with our mission for girls. It couldn't look like a typical recruitment advert—it had to be far more emotive. We 'um-ed' and 'er-ed' at one of those big meetings in our old office, discussing what would get people to come to an event and then join us. In the end it might have been my film-maker husband who poked me in the ribs and said, 'You guys are so boring—you need a more inspirational name for your volunteers!' And I knew he was right. We needed to build an identity and a real sense of belonging to something. And that something was obviously a team, and the purpose of this team was our girls! So we landed, quite simply, on 'Team Balika', Team for the Girl!

As we shifted gears into a big campaign, we were helped by this new name we had coined that enabled people to connect to us and our mission for girls. We no longer needed to use a term that other agencies or the government used for teaching assistants—'Shiksha Preraks'. We needed something where people engaged with the purpose rather than the idea of pay. Now we could really craft our invitations and our slogans. 'Join Team Balika and promote girls' education!' It was clear, inspiring and the start of building a team for the girl child.

In the weeks running up to our first event, we tried to understand all the existing communication channels in the most rural areas. What could we use that already existed, that communities already knew and trusted? This was of course way before the advent of WhatsApp groups and social media messaging, so we had to really look around and learn. On village walls, we found images selling fertilizers and cures for piles, all hand-painted. On billboards on the highway, we saw adverts for butter and ghee, for taps and toilet seats. The leaders of political parties often stared out at us from canvas posters strung across buildings. So we started to do the same. We commissioned local vendors who painted on average of three wall paintings per village and along the major roads and highways where buses carried commuters. We painted our phone number on these wall paintings and invited people to give us a missed call if they wanted to learn more. We didn't want money, the cost of a call, to be a barrier to them connecting with us—they needed to reach us for free. If anyone gave us a missed call, we called right back. The phones were so busy that we set up a well-resourced helpdesk to field them all and inform callers about our recruitment. We also put up posters in each village and distributed pamphlets (our photocopy vendor was kept very busy). Adverts were put in the local paper and our invitation was broadcast far and wide on the radio. The slogans were clear and simple—join our Team Balika, educate girls!

Next, we looked into more direct approaches. We leaned into our existing government partnership and wrote an old-fashioned letter, through the district administration, to village leaders and principals of the schools and junior colleges in the district. We informed them about our event and its purpose and gave presentations. We requested their support in inviting the right people to consider our opportunity. People who they felt were young, passionate, educated and wanted to join this mission.

Finally, we then got back into that Mahindra jeep again, but this time we had an enormous cone-shaped tannoy strapped to the front bumper like a beak between the two front lights. The vehicle looked like it had eyes! We had draped the jeep in banners and had an enormous black speaker on the roof. It felt like an election campaign. And as we drove through the villages, the importance of gilrs' education started to be heard as well as seen. Our team walked alongside the vehicle, engaging with onlookers, who would come out of their shops and houses to see what all the noise was about. And through this procession of sorts, we invited people to our very first recruitment meeting. Our aim was to ensure a good turnout of people on the day of the event. But would they come? Was it reasonable to expect people to turn up? We genuinely had no idea. And things didn't start well.

They Came and They Went

We had called people at 10 a.m. to the venue. Everything was set up and ready by about 9.30. The tent looked very inviting and Meena was just adjusting the final poster we had hung in the main room. Vikram tested the mic and speakers one last time and nervously sung us a quick couple of lines of '*Vande Mataram*' to confirm that everything was working okay. Next-door refreshments were also all laid out. Would fifteen people show up or fifty? We had decided to be optimistic and cater for many more, and I started to pour water into a few of the plastic cups with a slightly shaky hand. The wait had started. And although we were all pretending to be confident, furtive glances at our watches revealed quite now nervous we all were.

Then 10 a.m. came and went and no one appeared. By 10.30 a.m. only eight people had wandered in, looking a little bewildered as us, the Educate Girls team, outnumbered them two to one! Vikram suggested that we all get onto our phones and start ringing all those who had called us and said they would come. We didn't want people to feel in any way harassed, but as time ticked by we needed to know if anyone would indeed come! Perhaps one last call might encourage them. We worked our way through the lists and kept hearing the same response:

'*Ha ji*, we are on our way!'

Finally, at about 10.55 a.m. the local bus arrived from the other side of the block. I peered down the road to see if anyone would get off. To my astonishment, almost the entire, packed bus emptied out. Everyone was walking in our direction. A tempo (large rickshaw) then pulled up. More people got out. And then one by one, two-wheelers kicked up dust as they pulled on their brakes right outside the tent, some carrying two people, some carrying four! Three jeeps then rolled in and parked, and the noise levels started to rise. People were really coming!

It was extraordinary. By 11.15, the tent was full; in fact, it was bursting at the seams. I couldn't quite believe what had happened. People were seated in rows, but a seated body takes up more space than standing, so after ten or so rows, people were forced to stand as they crowded at the back of the tent. No meeting in Rajasthan, whether one-on-one or in a large group, was complete without a cup of tea, so, as usual, the smell of hot chai wafted across the crowd. I could smell cardamom and cinnamon and a caramelly hint of slightly overheated milk. I joined the team weaving in between the rows of bodies crowded onto the striped dhurries as we handed out chai and concertina plates made from old newspapers, filled with salty wafers—a delicious contrast to the very sweet tea. This suddenly felt like a mela—a village carnival. There were people everywhere. We had gathered under a large white-and-pink, two-roomed tent—one room for the proceedings, the other for the food.

A loud tap echoed around the tent. We were convinced we couldn't squeeze any more people in, so Vikram picked up the microphone and started welcoming everyone who had come.

He spoke about Educate Girls and our work and mission, and then Meena explained the importance of girls' education and talked more broadly about volunteerism and the idea of taking responsibility for the development of every village and, indeed, the nation. This was all powerfully illustrated by the Lead India film called *The Tree* (2010) that we showed on a large screen at the front of the tent. In the film, a tree fell across a busy road in a town. It appeared immovable as shopkeepers, rickshaw drivers, the police and other people looked on. Until a small boy, an unusual suspect, approached the tree and tried to push it himself. Inspired by his efforts, others joined in. Eventually, in the pouring monsoon rain, a big enough crowd, a big enough movement managed to move the tree! They celebrated their collective success and life carried on. It was a film that had been made and widely disseminated by *The Times of India*, trying to inspire citizen action to drive change across the country.[5] We hoped it might work for us too as we sought to persuade people they could play a role in changing their own village for the better.

As the proceedings paused, after the first part of the event, people started to get fidgety, and one or two people wandered out of the tent. Some had obviously just gone out to smoke a beedi, but others looked like they were preparing to leave. Earlier in the day, we thought no one would come to our event, then when they came, we worried everyone would leave!

Vikram immediately sprang to his feet and announced: 'If you are not interested, it is okay. However, we request that you stay back for lunch. We would not like anyone to leave before a full meal.'

The aroma of the hot food started to usurp the scent of the chai! We had ordered a veritable feast. Poori sabzi, rajma chawal and laddoos. The crowd slowly filed to the next-door tent. We fed everyone, perhaps in the hope they might stay—but really, we were determined to thank them, even if they didn't feel they were suitable for our team. I wanted to meet as many people as I could personally, so I circulated around during lunch. They had made the effort to come and listen to us. They had recognized the importance of talking about girls, so I wanted to meet them all, listen, and make sure we left no gap in our hospitality. But sadly, once everyone had finished eating and we tried to encourage them back into the main tent, they thanked us and left. The jeeps set off. The two-wheelers kicked up dust again. I thought a group was going to stay, but then realized they were waiting for a bus. All barring twelve of the 200 people left. But those twelve agreed to join us and we had learnt so much at this first event. And twelve people meant twelve villages. And twelve villages was a fantastic start—I tried to reassure the team that this was okay, and to some extent reassure myself!

On reflection it really was enough of a start, and by the time we had delivered two more events we had around a 60 per cent success rate in converting attendees to become part of Team Balika. We started our events later to make sure public transport aligned with our kick-off. We showed the Lead India film first, a communication that became the backbone of our recruitment until we raised money to make our own film, *Main Houn Team Balika* (I Am Team Balika) a few years later. And we made sure our helpdesk gave more information to all the callers from the advertisements so the volunteer message was received loud and clear before people turned up. Most importantly, we had some of our existing volunteers stand up and speak about themselves, their story and their experiences of volunteering with us and enrolling girls in school. Enthusiasm begets enthusiasm. Our most important allies and champions were indeed our existing team! They already felt part of something, and one of our most effective recruitment strategies was in the end our own people. When they rallied behind girls, others rallied too. When they stood up, others stood up too.

One by One They Stood Up

In every meeting after that, people turned up, and then one by one they stood up *for girls*. They were passionate individuals who aligned with our message stood up and shared their stories:

'A master's degree in arts has empowered me. I wish every girl in Rajasthan is able to get educated,' Nirmala from Rani district said confidently. Hers had been a long journey: Her mother was illiterate, she had had to fight to get to college, but she went on to join our team in Jalore district.

'I believe in the power of education, and I will help every girl in my village attain it.' This was how Jagdish explained his ambition. He had passed his twelfth grade but had seen his female cousins married at a very young age. Jagdish was from Rajsamund.

'It is my dream to see every girl from my village go to school,' said Sumer Singh from Sirohi. His sisters had not been allowed to go to school, but he had.

'My husband and children are proud that I am educated and I work to educate other girls in my village.' Varsha was a little older than a lot of the people who had spoken so far from her village. As the daughter of a schoolteacher, she had been lucky when most of her generation had not.

Instead of going to the village, the village came to us. This was how it went in our block and district meetings as the recruitment drive really took off. We started to see that we could reach a lot of people who thought like we did and that our messages touched a nerve. Our assertion that girls matter, that girls' education is vital was affirmed by women and men in the most unexpected places. People with stories came from every single village, looking for someone to listen and to give them an opportunity to turn their story into action. And that 'someone' was Educate Girls.

From a Few to a Great Many

Our campaign and recruitment events worked! In fact, we grew from 140 volunteers back in 2009 to over 1,000 in just three years. It surprised us that we managed to find so many people prepared to step forward. And as the numbers grew, they became a team, and as the team grew it became like an army, an army of gender champions, and that army became our 'Team Balika', our team for the girl child! But naysayers still existed.

'We can't find people to work for us in these villages, and we are the government!!' one district education officer warned us.

Nobody believed that the early success we had experienced, finding people to align with our mission and *give* their time to finding girls, would really be something we could deliver at scale. And it wasn't just the government officials in the district who had a hard time believing in us. New potential recruits would challenge this approach. They too questioned us. 'It might work for you in Pali or in Jalore, but it won't be possible in my district!' they would assert.

Perhaps it was unreasonable to expect people to join us. It was hard to make an argument to the government official who didn't believe us or to the new recruit in a fresh district who knew their community better than us, because in a way this did defy logic! On occasions, I doubted myself and our approach and thought that perhaps this time we wouldn't succeed. But I listened to my heart, and every time we did succeed! It was incredibly hard work, but our Team Balika was growing really, really fast. There was no rational reason why people were signing up in such numbers, but I left the rational and leant into the unreasonable.

My instinct that this was the right approach came from the fact that I had personally experienced what it felt like to have someone outside of my family get me back to school. My aunt Mahe had been like a Team Balika in my life. Why did she help me? She wasn't a social worker, she wasn't a teacher, and she was also not family—she was a *friend,* someone who stood beside me and supported me when I needed it. My time at school had been disrupted. People had lost their confidence in my education when I was out of school for over three years. I often struggled with traumatic memories from my earlier childhood, and when things got too overwhelming, I had to flee. And as I fled school, my parents despaired and reverted to default conclusions that as a girl I should forget about education and get married. They even lined a husband up for me—a divorcee with four children! They saw me as a problem and the solution was marriage. I shudder when I think that could have been my life, had my aunt not declared that I was not a problem, and that the solution for me was education.

She was there for me. She battled with these traditional views and battled with my parents. She knew me and knew my mind; she understood my potential and was prepared to swim against the tide with me. First, she persuaded me that I should go back to school. Then she persuaded my parents to support me with this decision, and then as time went on, she was the one who encouraged me to study even harder and apply to university in the UK. She got me back into the classroom, back to my studies, and I will forever be grateful to her for that. I now wanted this for every girl in every village. A friend, an advocate, an army of Mahes!

This was my story and a large part of why I am here today. And as we grew, I started to realize that it was not just my story. Everywhere we went, people understood what we were trying to do and told us about their own experiences and their own lives. They all had their own deeply personal reasons to fight for girls, and they explained this through their stories. We heard stories of overcoming family pressures, seeing siblings denied an education, experiencing how damaging illiteracy was to their mother or older sister. We heard stories of harsh in-laws, of unwanted girls. And then positive stories of going to school, of having a voice, of making progress in life. We then started to see that after working with us for a while, it was their storytelling that created the change in their village! The story of their life to date, and the future story they wanted to write for their village was why they stood up and joined us. It was this personal experience that I saw reflected in every member of Team Balika. In each and every one of them I saw the same kindness and sense of giving and purpose that I had seen in my aunt.

Intrinsic Motivation

The reason every Team Balika member worked so hard stemmed from deeply personal lived experience, a motivation to change their own village, and in doing so change themselves. Why did I get back on the plane from the US in 2004? This was my country and my problem. Similarly, we discovered that this is what motivated our volunteers.

'My village, my problem, and I am the solution. I will become a Team Balika!' This was their new rallying cry!

It might have been Anisha who first said this to me, or Kamlesh, Nadia Bano or Salma. Any number of our past or current volunteers might have been the ones to make this statement and inspire this powerful mantra, and over time it underpinned everything we did. 'My village, my problem, and I am the solution' became our Team Balika motto.

'It's our job to make people aware because it is our village. The development of our village lies in our hands,' one volunteer told me. And he went on to explain: 'When I see the children in the morning, they call me "Sir"—that is my identity now. Nothing makes me happier than seeing children learn because of me. People see me in the village and greet me. I now feel respected and that my work is important.'

'We have to make the change ourselves,' said Anisha. 'We cannot leave this to God!'

Our Team Balika were giving back a lot, working incredibly hard. But invariably they were quick to acknowledge what they were gaining for themselves. For Anisha Kumari, and other young women and men, the role of a village volunteer came with dramatically increased mobility and social interactions, not just through the work, but through the network of other volunteers who they trained with and shared peer support with. This was a hugely motivating factor. Anisha had been given certain freedom by her father, but was still quite tied to her home—always working with her father at home or in the fields after school, rarely socializing with girls her age, and studying remotely. Until she joined us at Educate Girls. Akelapan—loneliness—is very often cited by young girls as a deep feeling that has an impact on their lives, their confidence and mental health. Working with us was somewhat of a cure. Our young women were making friends through work. While the boys and young men played cricket whenever they wanted, many girls reported feeling criticized, frowned upon for playing or getting together with their friends. They felt they could only be at home. As her brother picked up his cricket bat after school every day, Anisha picked up a broom after school. They were even stored in the same place, leaning up against the wall. His and hers. Bat and broom. But volunteering with us allowed girls to legitimately play with the children, be out of the home and engaged with the world outside.

Babu Lal, an inspiring young man, had a similar experience. He was housebound because of a physical disability, had very few people in his life and, in a way, empathized with the situation of girls whose lives were so full of limitations. When he joined us, it was the first time he had left his village and travelled to the nearby town of Rajsamand for a training programme. His understanding of what it feels like to be dismissed, held back and confined to home was born out of experiences so similar to our girls. His enthusiasm for the work and the sense of belonging was infectious. 'With the other volunteers, I made friends; friends I had never had before.'

As we trained and supported them through our workshops, meetings and mentoring, our volunteers were bolstered by the skills and confidence they were building. Our training and their action was working. By going door to door, standing up in meetings and presenting, and speaking to government officials and school leaders, something big was starting to happen, personally for every one of them. Team Balika members reported a newfound self-assurance that enabled them to speak in front of crowds. There was almost always a before and after story of being shy, feeling invisible, and then after Educate Girls workshops and door-to-door survey realizing their passion through our work and discovering their voice.

'It [volunteering with Educate Girls] has given me a sense of self, elevated my stature in the village, and even at the block and district levels! There's no village in my block where people don't recognize me.'

Farzana, a fiery team member who I find it difficult to believe was once too shy to join our district meetings and speak up, said this. She can now command a crowd of a thousand people and persuade parent after parent to enrol their girls in school. 'If there's a new daughter-in-law in the village who wants to continue studying, the community contacts me for guidance. Today, the people in my village look up to me as a leader, and that's a responsibility I take pride in. That transformation has been the most fulfilling part of my journey.'

Farzana had managed to complete her ninth-grade exams, but only passed her tenth after an eight-year gap. She studied as an adult for her tenth because she wanted to work for girls. Because she wanted to join our team. Farzana was so driven to join Educate Girls and get girls in her community into education that she herself went back to school! She had once been the only girl in her village who travelled to the next village to go to school—which took a total of five hours travelling each day. And now, with her tenth-pass qualification in hand she is a local leader and a respected colleague.

As I met with more and more of our volunteers, and as the team was growing, their experiences took me right back to San Francisco, and the evolution of my own career out of the private sector and into nonprofits and my personal journey as a young woman. For me, it had also all started with volunteering. I knew deeply what it meant to give my time to a social cause and what volunteering had done for me.

Work in San Francisco was lonely. Hayes Valley in 1995 was a rough place. I lived just off the 101 ramps that was later torn down by the city, helping Hayes Valley re-emerge from its rough history to its new and current gentrified status. People on our street would leave their car doors unlocked and a clear sign on the windshield saying so, to prevent thieves from breaking the windows to steal the car radio. Windows were obviously more important or costly than radios! This was not something that had an impact on me as I have never learnt to drive. But it was a sign of the tensions in our neighbourhood back when I lived there.

From my tiny studio apartment, I would walk every day down Van Ness Street to catch a bus to Caltrain station and cram into the train to Santa Clara. If you missed it, you had to wait a full hour for the next one and then it took an hour to reach Silicon Valley. After that, I had to take a bus to my office. A bus that took me to a tiny cubicle next to teams of people coding all day. I was one of the only non-coders and one of the only people in my twenties, so it was a lonely existence. I had no friends in the city—I always got home too late to socialize. Nor did I have like-minded friends at work. I was new to the company and new to San Francisco and America and akelapan engulfed me too. So, after eight months, I cracked and begged my boss to allow me to stay in San Francisco one day a week and take up a volunteering role. Which he duly granted, much to my surprise.

My first stop was the Yellow Pages. I scoured the list of nonprofits with 'international' in their titles. I wrote to a shortlist, and rather than follow some onerous process of form-filling, I immediately joined an organization that worked in community development globally, including India, because they were the ones who phoned me up! In one conversation I was hooked—their mission spoke volumes given my heritage and experiences growing up in India. At their office in the Mission District, I met a group of young like-minded volunteers all around the same age as me. I had an immediate friend circle—peers who wanted to do the same thing as me brought together by purpose, by international development! I made friends with Becca, who had worked in Guatemala and just returned to the US. Tasha, who had spent a year abroad in Madurai, now wanting to help raise awareness and support in the US. Rachel and Martha were from England and passionate about social justice around the world. The work was meaningful. Figuring out how to raise funds to help women in South America buy sewing machines or set up a dairy cooperative in rural India or a project in the Philippines—this is what got me out of bed in the morning. Eventually, I quit my dotcom job to join the social sector full-time. Things then began to change, and I started my journey to where I am today.

Volunteering was the perfect platform to gain exposure and build the skills that have shaped me and my work over the years. It taught me how to build a network—a network that follows me today. I learnt the workings of the nonprofit sector, how to build and work in teams, problem-solving, maximizing resources and personally finding my own voice, decision-making ability and leadership. And this is what we gave our Team Balika: exposure, network and skills. Their journey mirrored my own, and in all of this I started to weave together their stories and mine, into the makings of a movement.

We Arrived at a Movement

'I don't feel like I work alone in this movement.' I loved how Farzana used the term!

A movement is essentially a delicate balance between spontaneity and organization. It is about each individual and their own motivation, but also about the collective, and this is what we began to see. As our Team Balika attended regular meetings, travelled out of their villages for training, and were supported through our helpdesk and connected to each other, they started to see they were no longer alone. There was someone just like them in the next village, and the next across their whole district. The sense of belonging to a tribe was strong and we worked hard to provide the 'glue' that helped them stick together. This group of colleagues, indeed *friends,* benefited every Team Balika member individually, but in coming together, bringing a spontaneous act into collective action, each individual joined together to become a movement. There was energy, power and inspiration in this coming together. They helped and supported each other, and as the news of their work spread, the reputation and respect they were gaining for themselves as local leaders and as Educate Girls also grew.

Everything we did just got bigger! We had bigger recruitment events, larger training programmes, and each year our annual foundation day celebration grew and grew. A sense of collective action for villages and blocks drove our Team Balika, until they could see that together they were having an impact on an entire district. But this was a quietly powerful movement, operating with sensitivity and tenacity across the thousands of villages where we worked. Our logo of the little girl with red pigtails was emblazoned on their shirts, their hats, their bags. Nothing fancy, no coat of arms or acronyms. Just the little girl, like a uniform and a badge of honour.

'Whenever people saw me with that bag, they would instantly recognize that I was part of Educate Girls, and that made me feel proud,' Farzana told me.

And this was just what we could see on the outside. More important was what they carried inside. Purpose, respect, a shared community goal. They started to look like a team, but critically, they felt like a movement—like they were part of something much, much more.

Putting purpose before everything else is an incredibly powerful way of working. Valuing the mission foremost ensures true engagement in community development, and it was clear from all the work we did to listen to and support our volunteers that they really were motivated by educating girls.

Was it unreasonable of us to expect this movement to evolve? Was it unreasonable of us to have had hope and persistence, to believe in the power of local voices and trust that enough people would come forward? Or had we actually just seized upon a natural desire for a new order that just needed a channel? Whatever the logic, we did it. We proved the district education officer who said we wouldn't find volunteers wrong. And we proved sceptical new recruits wrong as we expanded beyond Pali and Jalore, from Ajmer to Udaipur, from Bhilwara to Sirohi, from Jaipur to Rajsamand and then in 2015 over the border, beyond Rajasthan and into Madhya Pradesh, Uttar Pradesh and most recently Bihar! We did find people, we recruited them, trained them, brought them together as a movement, a movement that started to rewrite the story for girls.

Adapting to a world that remained fundamentally unequal for girls was not a solution I or any of our volunteers could accept. Those who joined me on this journey were relentless in their pursuit to adapt the world to them! Some thought we were unreasonable, but in our volunteers, we found tenacious young people, prepared to be just that. Unreasonable. By 2017 we had a movement of over 11,000 village volunteers and were working in 13,000 villages and were ready to dramatically scale up our work. Ready to find every last girl. We were growing, and this was an impressive scale for a community-based nonprofit. But with my growing understanding of the scale of the problem for girls, and my knowledge that we now knew what to do about it, my ambition and impatience got the better of me and I just knew we still had to move faster and not just grow at the current pace.

7

Moving at Speed

'If I were given one hour to save the planet, I would spend 59 minutes defining the problem and one minute resolving it,'

—Albert Einstein[1]

Imagine 11,000 passionate volunteers and team members, navigating dusty roads in and out of the villages, scaling the rolling hillsides of Rajasthan to make sure every hamlet is counted. They have notebooks, pens and mobile phones. They ask questions, listen, learn, and the stories they hear become the data that we analyse. Using GPS tracking, we are able to resource-plan, allocate people and set targets. We can support the teams better and also build accountability systems for our growing field teams and volunteers and reduce risk for their managers. Technology was enhancing our work. We knew that we had the right information and networks but I still had a growing sense of frustration that there was untapped potential and that we were going too slow.

The Village Lottery

Like ghosts they walked down the side of the road, caked in white dust from the construction site, carrying oversized kadais on their heads weighed down with gravel. This was back-breaking work in the scorching sun, and I only saw women—with their sarees hitched up and their dupattas across their mouths to stop them from inhaling the toxic clouds as they built the new national highway from Udaipur to Ahmedabad. These were the women of Jhadol block, where time had stood still. Cars very rarely reached the village we were visiting—there were perhaps four motorbikes, but most people moved about on bicycle or foot, making the slow 4-kilometre walk to the highway perhaps only once a week to then catch a tempo to the larger village 10 kilometres to the east. There they could find a small market and a branch of the State Bank of India. But here there was nothing. A large number of the men in the village had migrated to cities in search of work and the women were generally employed through the MGNREGA[2] scheme constructing this enormous new highway. Agriculture was the only other work in the village, but all small-scale, and only a few of the village members eked out any profit from their tiny strips of land. Subsistence farming was the norm.

A small and yet disbursed village, here we found a large number of out-of-school girls when we conducted our door-to-door internal survey in 2017. Just over the hill, on the other side of the National Highway construction site, was a similar sized village. Now, this other village had around a hundred households: families, mostly from the Dhakar (merchant) community who had a reputation for being good with money—salesmen, historically. There was little migration from this other village. The soil was good, irrigation was easy, with a good water table level, and despite an increasingly volatile climate, the crops thrived—wheat, gram, garlic, mustard, even peanuts. They were no longer really merchants, the village industry was agriculture and some daily labour work. But not many of the inhabitants of the village had to look outside it for work. It had its own shop and there was a small secondary school close by. The community here was well known locally for its mirrorwork, and this provided another source of income for the village families. It was also part of our door-to-door survey, but according to our list all the girls here were going to school.

We had been collecting door-to-door data for nearly ten years, and over time we had become more and more focused on supporting our Team Balika and field teams with the tools to speed up their work and the numbers they needed to make decisions. Decisions that would help the programme become increasingly effective and help us find more girls. They were already equipped with GPS mapping and a mobile phone app that helped them plan and collect data, and help us resource-plan and ensure accountability. But we had never really zoomed out and looked at all our data with a different level of analysis. But this year, inspired by some deep analysis we were doing with the evaluators of one of our district projects, we were indeed looking at all our data differently, and we realized that the magnitude of these numbers was starting to tell us a story. Specifically, we started to see a cluster effect. On the south side of the NH road construction, we were finding a lot of out-of-school girls across the villages, hundreds in fact. On the northside, far, far fewer. A handful in one or two villages. What we saw was a geographical lottery. In this particular block, if you were born on one side of the highway you might go to school; on the other side, you would likely not. Where you were born could dictate everything, particularly if you were born a girl.

As an organization, Educate Girls was also playing and losing at this lottery as we continued, unwittingly, to allocate resources to villages where we found very few out-of-school girls, sometimes none. There was of course a celebration when we found that all girls were in school, but we knew that there were villages where the opposite was the case and we needed to get to those villages a lot faster. As we rolled out our programme we would find a Team Balika member in every village, allocate a paid field coordinator to every ten villages, conduct a full door-to-door survey of the whole district and run regular meetings. Then, in some villages, all girls were in school! We put the same team and effort into both these villages. In one village, we found thirty out-of-school girls. In the other none. There had to be a different way—a faster way to find the villages where the problem was most acute.

Getting There Faster

It was now September 2017, and after my visit to Jhadol block, I had taken a break from field operations for a few weeks and was in the US to shortly join the chaos or excitement (depending on how you look at it) that is the UN General Assembly in New York. I had flown from India via the west coast to catch up with my old friends in San Francisco. It felt great to be back. But I had a lot on my mind.

San Francisco also happened to be the home of the advisory, data analytics and research organization IDinsight, who were conducting the evaluation I mentioned of our work in the district of Bhilwara. It had been quite a challenging year so far as we simultaneously expanded into new districts and coped with the pressure of the Bhilwara project. We were now supporting and mentoring an 11,000-strong Team Balika army and, on top of everything, in just a few months we would be celebrating our tenth foundation day. We wanted to celebrate by throwing a really big event and write a decadal impact report!

IDinsight's lofty, air-conditioned office was a far throw from the dust and heat where I had been working in Rajasthan just a week earlier, and also far from where I had lived in Hayes Valley or 7th and Minna, for that matter. But as I sat and waited for Buddy Shah, the founder, I was put at ease by a wily dog who had decided to sit next to me in the meeting room and nudge my elbow with his long, wet nose. 'On my way', my phone informed me as the text message buzzed on my thigh and surprised the dog.

We had planned the meeting in order to take a deeper look at our data and discuss learning from the recent evaluation results. We only had a year left on the three-year funding contract and still had 50 per cent of our goal to reach.[3] We needed to see if the numbers could tell us anything about how to accelerate our progress in the final year. As Buddy bustled into the meeting room, pulled up a chair and joined me at the table, the meeting started to go in a very different direction as I shared some of my disappointment at what I saw as the slow pace of our work.

'I have done some calculations based on our progress over the last decade, Buddy, and if we carry on at this rate, too many girls will miss out on an education—we will lose this generation,' I explained. 'It's just too slow!'

Buddy paused. He didn't immediately make any suggestions but posed the question: 'What is your biggest problem to solve?' Now Buddy should really be addressed as Dr Neil Shah, if I am to use his correct title. It is not often that you meet a qualified physician, who also has an economics degree and a list of affiliations that include Harvard University, Harvard Kennedy School, MIT's JPal, the World Bank and the list goes on. To compliment his title, Buddy was as elegant and handsome as his stature demanded! He sits at the intersection of data science and human development, and if anyone can integrate the two successfully it's Buddy, and he is a great one for asking the right question!

'It is quite simple, Buddy,' I replied and then paused in order to compose myself. 'There are just so many girls in India who aren't going to school, but we know they are no longer everywhere. We seem to be carpet-bombing with our programme, but the problem is uneven—there are villages where all the girls are now going to school. But then there are hotspots where we are finding many, many out-of-school girls in one village. These are the clusters we need to find quicker. I want to find every last girl who is being denied an education. Once we find her we know what to do to get her into school and learning. But my problem is there are just so many girls, and not enough time and not enough money. And it's such a huge country! Perhaps what I really need to know is where to look.'

And then what came tumbling out was the promise and yet the pain points of our ten-year history! We had started in Pali district in 2007 and now had teams of Team Balika volunteers across thirteen districts of India, spreading across Rajasthan and now into neighbouring Madhya Pradesh. Up until today, our approach had been a strategy of 100 per cent saturation of government-identified critical gender gap districts. These districts are large, anywhere from 500 villages to 2,000-plus villages. To ensure we found every last girl, we would knock on every single home in the district. The sums were mind-boggling. Every home in a 1,000-village district might add up to as many as 1,00,000 houses, and knocking on every door might take us six years at our current rate. We needed a different approach. As the surveys were completed and patterns emerged, we started to see that in a large number of villages all the girls were indeed going to school. Indeed, at one point we concluded that around 20 per cent of our villages didn't have a single out-of-school girl, and yet we had still knocked on every door in that village to check, expending time and expending hard 'raised' resources. And then at the same time we would have team members find an overwhelming 100 girls in one village, an unmanageable number for one person! It all seemed so unpredictable.

Questions and Answers

If artificial intelligence is the answer—what is the question?

'We're not the government, Buddy,' I finally concluded with an air of resignation, stating the obvious but also repeating a phrase my team had used a few years prior to question my aspirational plans to start our own census! 'We don't have unlimited resources. Hiring large teams, training and safeguarding is a huge undertaking—I just feel like there must be a quicker, better, more cost-effective way of doing all this!'

What I didn't expect next was what felt, at the time, like a totally futuristic and 'sci-fi' suggestion. What we were about to dig into was artificial intelligence. AI is now a commonplace topic of conversation that has people consumed by either fear or excitement depending on their knowledge, temperament or world view. But back in 2017, it was much less understood and there were little to no conversations about its application in the social sector. For me, it was very abstract and it felt far, far removed from our work, our villages and our girls. At Educate Girls, we had embraced technology as a necessary and creative tool in the toolbox, we had GPS tracking for our teams, we used smartphones and dashboards, but we had also embraced all this with deep thought and with a healthy scepticism, knowing that nothing could replace human trust, human being and human intelligence! But Buddy had other ideas. He asked me again, 'What is the problem you want to solve, what is your greatest challenge?'

My answer was, 'My greatest challenge is this—I need to get to the villages with the highest number of vulnerable girls as fast as possible. I wish we could just *predict* where we would find those villages!' The more energetic and frustrated I sounded, the calmer and more composed Buddy became, and then a light bulb went on in his mind!

'The minute Safeena used the word "predict", it dawned on me that this was a classic machine-learning challenge,' Buddy recalls.

We had been ensconced in the meeting room at the IDinsight office for well over an hour now. The office, funnily enough, was a pretty nondescript building in downtown San Francisco that eight years later would be sandwiched just ten minutes from where the world's two biggest AI labs would establish their headquarters! Lalu the dog had wandered off to find another lap to lean on and Buddy poked his head out of the door and started waving his hand at a colleague perched on a bright-coloured sofa on the other side of the loft who was just within earshot.

'Ben,' he hollered, 'you have to come over here and meet Safeena.'

Ben Brockman was an expert data scientist on the team whom I had not met before. He was usually based in Washington so it was by fluke that he happened to be visiting San Francisco that day. As Ben made his way over, Buddy continued: 'This is all about prediction!'

It was a classic challenge that machine learning was incredibly well-placed to solve, if and only if you had the right data. Companies used machine learning to inform their expansion plans, Buddy went on to explain. It helped them decide where to build supermarkets or distribution centres, or what demand for a product might be at a particular time of year in order to plan production. Ride apps use machine learning to predict when there will be surges in customers needing a ride—such as Saturday nights, when it is raining or when the cinema closes, for example. There is no reason why we couldn't do this to find out-of-school girls! Forecasting the future based on the past.

At the time, this type of data science was also new to IDinsight and Ben was their first hire to focus on it in earnest. He had worked at IDinsight a few years earlier, but had gone off to Harvard Kennedy School to complete his MPA, and then thrown himself into the Clinton campaign, anticipating a role at the White House after the fated election. As Hillary lost the election, Ben had made his way back to IDinsight to launch the data science component of the organization. When Ben told me that his policy thesis at Harvard had looked at how to use machine learning to predict school dropouts in Rwanda, I was quite blown away by how aligned his experience was going to be. First, we had a census for girls, now we were talking about an algorithm, I thought to myself! I was pretty blown away.

We sat for another hour, 'wonking out', as Buddy likes to say—talking in tech speak. On some occasions, my mind wandered off and I looked over to Buddy's team as colleagues got up from their computers sporadically to chuck a basketball into the full-size net in the tiny courtyard. What went on in those computers again felt detached from the reality faced by our girls and our villages, but despite the fact that Ben and Buddy were talking in what seemed like a foreign language at times, I understood the potential was enormous. We were going to move from carpet-bombing to precision-targeting!

After I left the meeting their words were just buzzing around in my head. We had been so wedded to our door-to-door survey—it had seemed like it was the only way to find every girl. But we needed to take bolder action, become more strategic and get to the right village, to a majority of girls *faster*! Was artificial intelligence the crystal ball we needed?

Teaching a Machine to Learn

So how do you teach a machine? How does a machine learn? The key is the data you put in to train the machine to think or predict for itself. Past data is used to predict the future. Taxi apps use traffic data to predict how long you might have to wait for a car, streaming apps use customer history to predict what music someone might want to listen to next. In our case we thought we might be able to use data about families, villages and schools that the government had to predict where out-of-school girls might live. The key to this was having a lot of data about out-of-school girls and where they *actually lived* before we got started, and that was precisely what we had as a result of our years of work and our extensive door-to-door survey!

Buddy and Ben waited to learn more about the data with a tinge of scepticism, as it is incredibly rare for an NGO to have the kind of datasets that would really allow prediction through machine learning. After our exciting meeting, I had left San Francisco for New York and got caught up with events and meetings but, as promised, within the week I was able to get Buddy's team and mine together over a call to discuss what we had. In the first conversation, we shared the kind of data we had collected for one of our districts.

Then Ben, impressed, but still a little uncertain, asked me: 'Could you give me a sense of approximate *total* numbers? How many homes have you actually surveyed and got the data for altogether?' Ben was perhaps trying to manage his expectations a little.

But when I replied a few days later from my little hotel room in New York with the exact figures that equated to close to 1 million households, Ben got the answer he wanted. We had enough data to train the machine. We had a list of out-of-school girls across close to 8,000 villages. Ten years of painstaking work by our field teams and Team Balika was the gold mine they were looking for. Ben said, 'And what was amazing was that the data was already organized.' Like I say, I love a tidy list!

'The team in India literally had all the data that was needed to do the training of the machine—all the technical stuff—and, if we went on to execute, the impact upside was just way better than we could possibly have imagined,' Buddy recalled. It was a story that still energized him today!

Apparently, there are a lot of applications of machine learning that are not all that consequential and only really sound good on paper, not necessarily improving impact all that much. But after just the first rough cut of our data, Buddy's team was able to see that we had an opportunity to predict and find close to half the primary-aged out-of-school girls in India. Now that was HUGE.

Predictable Girls

What IDinsight did next, in that loft office in San Francisco with Lalu the dog under their desks, was 'scrape' what is called 'predictor variables/data' from publicly available sources for 7,796 villages, chosen because we had been there recently and knew the actual number of out-of-school girls in each and every village. What were the literacy levels, caste or tribe status, average family size, occupations and school infrastructure like in the villages with the most out-of-school girls? The machine crunched all this data and learnt where the correlations were between the girls' context and whether or not they were enrolled in school. The machine looked and it learnt.

Deciding what predictor data was most relevant for our girls was the next puzzle. What would really help us predict whether a girl would go to school, or more precisely, predict that a parent was unlikely to enrol their girl in school? Was it her parent's literacy levels? Was it her proximity to the school? Was the parents' income a factor or the fact that she was from a particular community? What made a girl 'predictable'? A girl who was predictably out of school?

As the team started to examine the data, all those names came flooding back to me. They were data points for the machine. For me they were all stories. They were all lives. 'Antimbala' is a predictable girl. Her parents are illiterate; they are from an OBC (Jats) in Rajasthan. Antimbala is from a relatively big family—with three daughters born before her and the much-awaited brother Raj Kumar, born five years after her. Her father works away at the brick kiln over the border in Gujarat. Her mother manages the tiny strip of land they rent which provides some basic produce to the family, with only a very small onion surplus to sell. The school in the village is very poorly attended. The girls' toilet is poorly maintained, the powercuts are long and the secondary school is very far. All this adds up to Antimbala not going to school.

Maafi (sorry) is a predictable girl. Sorry she is the eldest of four girls, sorry she is from the Mahyavanshi caste, sorry her father died of a heart attack. Faltu (useless) is a predictable girl. But she is far from useless. It is her father really who deserves the 'useless' label, sadly spending most of the day inebriated. Neither of her parents have consistent work. She is from the Bhil tribe, and without steady income Faltu is usually forced to work in the agarbatti factory. She is the oldest girl in the family, the school is far and she is predictably out of school.

To improve the predictions over time, we needed to decide what predictor data we would use. What did we think were the root causes of girls not going to school? What were the barriers to girls accessing their right to education? What were the reasons why Antimbala was at home and not with her brother in the classroom? What did we need to know that might help us predict where to find the most out-of-school girls?

What was very helpful at this stage in the evolution of our work was that the team in San Francisco understood India. Ben and Jeff, another colleague, had lived and worked in Bihar—the state in India with some of the most challenges for women and girls. They had a deep knowledge of the context of our work, and had even brought their dog back to the United States from India! As they 'cleaned their data' and ran the numbers they sat beneath inspirational quotes from Mahatma Gandhi and knew the meaning behind what they were looking at. It wasn't news to them that twelve-year-old girls were married, that schools often had no toilets, that parents' literacy rates were so low and that child labour was pervasive. They could ask the right questions and understand what the numbers might be telling us.

We gathered opinion from education, gender and development experts, combined it with our deep knowledge of our communities and narrowed the predictors down a bit, but still fed over 313 indicators into the machine. All data that was free and accessible and from trusted sources.

The most comprehensive dataset was of course the Indian census, and from this we selected 233 indicators. What were the literacy levels in a village? An illiterate parent was undoubtedly a solid predictor that a girl might be out of school. We included religion, caste, employment status and household income. The size of a household was also a clear indicator—the bigger the family, the higher the likelihood of out-of-school girls. We included the presence (or not) of a toilet in the house, the source of water—tap or well—and we even input what kind of roof a family had over their heads,—pukka or kutcha. On top of this, 118 indicators came from the District Information System for Education where data points such as gross enrolment rates, girls' enrolments, school governance and whether the school included the secondary grades were used. The more data the better.

(Hu)man vs Machine

Once we had taught the machine it was then time to test the predictions. In the first year, Vikram—by then our expansion lead and senior manager—and his team already had a set plan of where they wanted to expand our programmes. So, fuelled with some healthy scepticism and a determination not to put all our eggs in one basket, rather than being led by machine learning, they carried on with their survey based on their own contextual knowledge and village selection. Simultaneously Buddy, Ben and Jeff ran predictions on those same villages. When the predictions were shared internally after the survey was completed, the findings surprised everyone. The tool was working much better than anticipated, and after just one iteration of the model we realized the machine was able to help us to find between 50 per cent more girls in some villages and a staggering 100 per cent more girls in other villages.

Over time, the machine has become more and more accurate at predicting where we will find the most out-of-school girls, where Antimbala, Faltu and Maafi are likely to live. It won't tell us exactly how many girls we will find in a village. It won't tell us which house, but what it will do is take a district and give us an idea of where there will be a concentration of villages with high numbers of out-of-school girls. It tells us relatively accurately if a village is likely to have above-average or below-average numbers of out-of-school girls so we can take decisive action about where to work. So we avoid villages where the machine says we will likely find less than ten girls who don't go to school and go where the machine tells us we will likely find more than fifty out-of-school girls. When we first started working in this way, we were finding on average eighteen girls in every village we decided to go to. After a few years and refinements to the algorithm we were finding close to forty-two girls per village—demonstrating that we were getting better and better at our predictions and going where the problem was greatest.

'We really think you should go here,' Ben said as his finger landed on a very dark part of his immaculate computer-generated map, a very different document to our hand-drawn village maps. We sat down with Ben on one of his visits to Mumbai. He and his team had been working hard on the latest map of clusters and were still negotiating their way around the operations team in India and their sensible suspicion.

'Ah,' Vikram would respond with a slight 'told you so' resignation. 'There is a mountain range just there—that will take a field coordinator around five days to cross. Those villages can't be in this cluster!'

Ben paused and tried again. 'Well, this is an obvious area here,' he proposed, hoping that another geological barrier would not emerge from the page.

'Ah,' Vikram responded again with a hint of schadenfreude. 'There is a particularly difficult district education officer there. We have tried, but I doubt we will ever be able to work in those villages. He doesn't like us!'

I would observe these interactions with intrigue and hope. And, of course, beneath all of this were ethical and practical questions. Just because the machine predicted something, it didn't mean we could always follow through. We needed to find talent, we needed the government to agree, we needed there not to be a mountain in the middle of a village cluster! This was a hugely productive creative tension that over time delivered better and better results. Over the course of a decade, we first put our Team Balika in place at massive scale and then integrated smart technology to make their job easier. People ask me about the ethics of a machine telling us where to work, but nowhere does a machine replace a human when it comes to individual girls. The machine just tells the people where to go for maximum impact. The balance of human intelligence with artificial intelligence is the winning combination, and this approach has the potential to accelerate social change across a multitude of sectors.

We had spent ten years demonstrating that we could target a district and go to every village and every household to find out-of-school girls. We had demonstrated that we could not only find girls, but also sustainably enrol them in school, and—something I haven't even mentioned yet—we were also significantly improving learning outcomes for all the girls and boys in schools where we worked. Having said all this, however, if we wanted to find Antimbala, every last girl, *quicker*, we needed to work out which of India's villages would have the most out-of-school girls, and only look there! And now we had an algorithm to make it happen!

The government data was telling us there were over 4.1 million primary-aged, out-of-school girls in India[4]. This became our universe and our north star. Overwhelming numbers can encourage apathy in some; but to me they are a red rag to a bull. Another important figure is this—85 per cent of India's schools are in villages, and 74 per cent of India's children live in rural India. If there are 4.1 million out-of-school girls, the majority, we could assume, will live in villages. We needed a unit of expansion and India's soulful villages were the obvious answer.

The 2011 census data—which was and still is the most comprehensive dataset available to us, and from where we drew our predictor data—had counted just over 6,40,000 villages. (If each village was only a couple of miles across and you positioned them next to one another they would wrap around the earth thirteen times!) As we sat there under the Gandhi quote in the IDinsight office, 'Be the change you want to see in the world', and in the process of all this data analysis and machine-learning design, we had a huge eureka moment. If you gather enough data, you start to see patterns, and what we were seeing was that in the majority of villages, like Agarpura, we were finding just one or two girls who weren't going to school, sometimes none—in fact, almost half the villages we went to had only one or two girls. When Ben and Buddy drew this up in a graph, we could see that close to 40 per cent of all our out-of-school girls were living in just 5 per cent of the villages we had visited. This was a concentration problem, no longer universal. Of the 6,40,000 villages in India we only needed to go to 30,000. Finally, this seemed like a manageable number. As our saturation census-like approach unravelled, a new, more targeted possibility emerged. The model was making it all the more imperative that we worked out *where to look*!

'If we can confidently assume that 40 per cent of the out-of-school girls live in just 5 per cent of the villages, I believe we can teach a machine to tell us which villages we need to go to!' Ben announced. Teaching a machine to predict areas of such vulnerability, where that marginalization and negative mindset intersect, has the potential to be game-changing.

An out-of-school girl can be a proxy for poor malnutrition, prevalence of child marriage, incidence of gender-based violence and vulnerability to child trafficking or child labour. Finding every last girl has a huge multiplier effect, and so anything we can do to find her faster deserves this human and technological effort!

Combination Therapy

Our next five years were spent delivering on this audacious goal, and putting our movement and our machine learning into practice to unlock the huge multiplier effect that is girls' education. One thing I really want to emphasize here is that all this human and technological effort was also accelerated by the tailwind we experienced as government efforts gained huge momentum during this period. Our movement of Team Balika members, guided by the machine-learning predictions, had a much easier job once they reached a village because of our alignment with government policy. Progress that was being made at the system's level, to build incentives and financial support for the families who had previously been left behind, acted like combination therapy—the right dose of community action, civil society programming and government policy started to deliver.

The physical barriers dissolved as the RTE mandated a school within 1 kilometre of every village. This meant that the mantra 'the school is too far' no longer held. Our Team Balika volunteer's job was focused far more now on mindset than the distance to school. Economic marginalization, of course, still reared its head, but here the Rajasthan government put schemes in place to support families financially. The Mukhyamantri Rajshri Yojana (MRY) was one such scheme, applicable for girls born in or after 1 June 2016. This offered a mother $600 over the course of a daughter's first eighteen years and was linked to milestones like institutional birth, full vaccination and then enrolment and transition through the four stages of school, essentially incentivizing good health practices and every girl's presence in school.

Perhaps most significantly of all was Beti Bachao, Beti Padhao, also launched at this time (2015), that after years of denial acknowledged the existence of widespread son preference, a societal blight that we have discussed in such harrowing depth earlier. All of a sudden this initiative saw slogans and placards, posters and films on billboards, the back of rickshaws and buses, in cinemas and the internet, and across the length and breadth of the country—with Prime Minister Narendra Modi spearheading the movement, and politicians fronting social media campaigns with selfies with their daughters. It may seem slightly trite, but it worked, and all this communication and elevation of the importance of girls, this acknowledgement that girls and boys are treated differently, made a huge contribution to our work. We had the law to back up our enrolment drives and we had this groundswell of messaging that amplified a girl's right to be safe and to thrive through education. The biggest, most complex barrier of them all, namely, mindset, was finally being tackled head on.

This combination of government policy with grassroots individual and community action, merged with technology, accelerated our pace of work and delivered on an 'audacious' plan to support the enrolment of 1.5 million out-of-school girls across 5 per cent of India's villages back into school or into a classroom. Finally, we were working at speed!

8

The Multiplier Effect

'Investment in girls' education may well be the highest return investment available in the developing world.'

—Lawrence Summers, World Bank Chief Economist, 1992[1]

A billion-dollar business is known as a unicorn. In the social sector 'an impact unicorn or a social unicorn'[2] is one that has the potential to reach millions of people with their work, creating social change at massive scale. It's a term that has been used for Educate Girls—an achievement I am immensely proud of.[3] So, what is the end goal for this scale and growth? What has this journey been for? Why do we want to help girls get back into schools and classrooms where they belong? What is this so-called multiplier effect of girls' education?

One Girl Can Change a Village

'What has changed in the last decade or so?' I asked her when we met her recently.

'*Bahut!* [A lot!]' she replied with a twinkle in her eye and a wide, wide smile.

I want to now take you back to Andu, whom we met back in 2010 when her daughter was two years old. As I explained, Andu was educated. Having escaped from a restrictive marriage and in-laws who threatened to kill her daughter, Andu owed so much to her education. She would likely not have had the presence of mind to escape if she hadn't been to school and held on to the confidence that studying and learning to read had given her. Perhaps she would not have understood the injustice and recognized the abuse she was suffering if it hadn't been for her time in school. Andu's education meant that she questioned her mother-in-law's instructions to take ash from the fire, mix it in water and feed it to her newborn. Andu knew this was murder. She knew it was in her power to prevent this from happening. And she did.

It must have been tough living the life of a single woman. But after her escape, Andu moved back to her native village. She brought her daughter up on her own and then used her education to cause a ripple effect across her village and beyond. Andu joined our movement and worked in a further cluster of villages that we knew were hotspots of vulnerability for girls through our predictive analytics. A decade later, Andu works as an upsarpanch[4] as well as a programme coordinator with Educate Girls.

Not just in her own village, but across the eleven villages in her ward, not one single girl has been out of school for many years now. This is unusual for Banswara, a deeply forested district and home to a majority tribal population. Banswara, possibly named 'bans vara' or 'land of bamboo', is the southern-most district in Rajasthan and lies in the Mahi River basin bordering Madhya Pradesh. People in Banswara suffered from a lack of infrastructure, and the district was selected as one of 250 districts—back in 2007—in need of investment to redress this imbalance, so up until 2014 it was part of the government's Backward Regions Grant Fund programme.[5] But it is now the norm in this area for girls to go to school. Girls go to school and women read. And by reading, women are learning, among other things, improved farming practices. Andu proudly spoke of how women were leading the change in her village and through learning how to care for their goat and cattle herds better, with the latest animal husbandry techniques, the milk production had increased tenfold!

'*Auroton ko abhi jyada rozgar milta hai!*' Andu explained proudly. Women are engaged in more employment now.

It was now the norm for women to work either in or outside the home. And work at home was also very different. Thriving enterprises had made working at home more fruitful and usurped time spent on unpaid household chores. These chores were of course still essential, but beyond that, the majority of Andu's fellow ladies in the community ran small businesses. They were connected to the local economy. They knew where and for how much to sell their papad (poppadom) and paper bags.

Andu's observations in her village about the multiplier effect of education are not just anecdotal or observational.

In the years that we have been working, the evidence base has grown stronger and stronger. So you don't need to take my word for it! Whereas back in 2007 we had to make the case for investing in girls, argue for a girls' right to equality and inclusion, today this is no longer the case, and academics the world over have been studying this and explaining it. Putting the numbers behind our stories. Their research illustrates the fact that investing in girls' education is one of the best investments a country can make.

'*Jyada rozgar* [more employment]' was how Andu described what she had seen across her villages. And she is convinced this is because the community now sends their girls to school. The rate of return on each additional year of schooling for girls has been consistently estimated to be a 10 per cent increase in wages, with higher returns for girls completing secondary education.[6] Imagine the impact that has on a woman in Andu's village. The income that she can earn compared to that of her mother is extraordinary. In a generation, so much can change, and not just at a village level, but nationally. In a study of 100 countries it was found that increasing the share of women completing secondary education by 10 per cent increases economic growth by 3 per cent—which is a significant amount.[7] Andu can see this in the income of women in her community—in what her friends and neighbours take home each week or each month. And when we zoom out, if 100 per cent upper secondary completion rates were achieved by 2030,[8] on average the national GDP could see an uplift of 10 per cent according to analysis across eight countries by Plan International and Citi Global. This could see between $15 trillion and

$30 trillion added back into the global economy—now that is a huge multiplier![9]

Andu's cluster of villages was doing visibly better. And, if needed, government schemes were accessed. Knowledge was known and shared. And, to that end, bribes were not always necessary. Andu's community knew how to access schemes without the need for a bribe, and the middlemen found it harder to make an extra buck. The community was not only economically more productive but healthier too. Andu explained that institutional births were now the norm. She had seen how babies' lives were saved as educated women gave birth in a hospital or accessed community medical support. This was backed up by global research too. A study of child mortality in 175 countries from 1970 to 2009 found that increases in women's education were responsible for more than half the reduction in under-five child mortality. That's 4.2 million lives saved because of girls' education.[10]

Goal-setting

As we came out of the Millennium Development Goals (MDG) era in 2015 and seventeen new Sustainable Development Goals were agreed upon, this kind of evidence was used to identify targets and the measurement of the progress that we were making towards a 'better world' by 2030. As we at Educate Girls were busy gathering our evidence of change, globally, the world was also starting to research and quantify the impact that girls' education was having on many of the indicators identified. Academicians agreed that girls' education could help save 11 million babies from dying before their fifth birthdays[11] and save 12 million children from stunting through malnutrition if SDG goals were met.[12] Girls' education would prevent women from dying in childbirth[13] and from contracting HIV. But how? Academicians could demonstrate this and we saw it for ourselves. Educated women are much better placed to access and negotiate life-saving healthcare for both themselves and their children,[14] more likely to vaccinate their children, give birth in a hospital, use a bednet—the list goes on.[15] This may all sound overwhelming, but again, a lot of this was seen first-hand by Andu in her village. Families were noticeably smaller, and children noticeably healthier. The more girls educated the better, but *more education for each girl*, even better—research was showing us that universal *primary* education for girls could reduce child mortality rates by 15 per cent; if we give every girl a *secondary* education the reduction is as much as 49 per cent![16]

We must also consider how recently rampant gender inequality and child rights abuses were still acceptable in Europe. The Education Act of 1870 was a turning point in England and similarly in the United States, but throughout the Industrial Revolution children were working long hours in factories, particularly in the textile industry, in agricultural settings and down mines. In the early twentieth century, in both the US and the UK, around 50 per cent of girls were enrolled in elementary school—far less likely to continue into secondary school.[17] But gender norms have also taken their time to change, and cultural practices have often not kept pace with policy, particularly in rural communities the world over. And India isn't always an outlier.

When Women Make Decisions

With Andu's role as upsarpanch, her story is one of political leadership and decision-making. Women 'pass it on', as they say. Their education is not just something they hold on to for themselves or their own family, they use it for others too. Research shows that correlating census data on literacy, and matching that with electoral outcomes shows that narrowing the gender literacy gap raises women's participation as voters and candidates in politics.[18] And when educated women are more engaged in the democratic process, governments and institutions globally are less corrupt! Gender parity breeds better democratic process.[19] If we take this to the village level, a study across 265 village councils in India showed that villages where leadership positions were reserved for women invested more in the development priorities expressed by women such as in water and education.[20] This is exactly what I learnt from Andu. Working as an upsarpanch, she not only ensured that women benefitted, but that everyone did.

The protection of the law is so much more effective when women are educated—they know their rights, can navigate schemes and see through corruption. Educated women are more likely to report domestic violence and stand up to discrimination. The International Labour Organisation has studied this.[21] When a girl realizes her right to an education, she then realizes she has other rights to fight for!

Finally, it is clear that education begets education. I don't think that in all my years I have met an educated mother who has denied her own daughter an education, or her son, for that matter. The Indian Institute of Management (IIM) Ahmedabad conducted a study that shows that if mothers have at least some level of education, children (especially girls) are more likely to attend school, stay in school longer, and perform better academically.[22] Andu's educated peers are all sending their children to school. And with that, change happens.

People and the Planet

It is the evidence of a multiplier effect that has justified our hurry to educate girls, our belief in the need for both speed and scale. John Doerr, in his book *Speed & Scale: An Action Plan for Solving our Climate Crisis Now*,[23] who made such a strong case for the urgency with which we need to be addressing the climate crisis, included girls' education as a solution. It is of course first vital to recognize that, as I have mentioned before, women and girls are disproportionately impacted by the climate crisis. This makes the case for more and better girls' education even stronger, as research concludes that higher education levels for girls can contribute to increased resilience in the face of natural disasters. Academics have gone so far as to say that deaths due to disasters could be reduced by 60 per cent if a significant portion of young women (70 per cent) completed lower secondary school.[24] 'Female education is the single most important social and economic factor associated with a reduction in vulnerability to natural disasters' is what a study of 130 countries concluded![25]

If we go back to our human rights discussion, the right to twelve years of education alongside the right to access free family planning will undoubtedly see a large reduction in the global population. By 2050, with an educated global population and the right to choose when to have a baby, it is clear that unwanted pregnancies will reduce dramatically, and smaller family size will be the norm. If the world's population grows by 8.4 per cent *less than current predictions*, there would be a reduction of 70 gigatons of GHG emissions, so this has to be a good thing.[26] If rightfully women choose their family size, they are choosing a better life for themselves and a huge positive upside for the planet.

Education Just for Her

So, there we have it—the people in positions, that people think 'matter', passionate academics, economists, development practitioners, the G7,[27] even, have all confirmed that the evidence is there: Girls should be educated so that there is widespread global-, national-, village- and family-level impact for others. An educated girl can influence so much, and her education is so powerful. But the more I make this argument the more I disassociate from what I am saying and realize I am falling into a trap of patriarchy. Why should a girl be educated for somebody else? My education was mine. Why should an investment in her education be contingent upon a multiplier, be argued for and justified by her impact on another, rather than a change, a power, a voice and a choice for her? Just for her?

I, of course, applaud all these arguments and trust and appreciate all the mounting evidence, as this gives me an additional narrative to support everything I already innately know. This means you don't have to just take my word for it. But having said all this, these arguments and intersections anger me as well. As I see it, they are proof that the world is still captured by a patriarchal mindset.

If a girl's worth lies primarily in her ability to contribute to others rather than herself, if her value is in the service of others rather than intrinsic and recognized as her own, then I fear that we haven't moved on enough to truly believe in every last girl as an individual.

9

The Meaning of an Education

'I learnt to write so I can write my fate.'

—Young learner at an Educate Girls Pragati Camp, November 2024

The only true reason to educate a girl is that it is her right. When a girl articulates what her education means to her, we will undoubtedly still hear her speak with a residue of the inequality she has lived with. She might explain her education through the lens of the cultural and social norms we are seeking to change. But we will also hear what I hope is a compelling argument about why girls' education matters, why their lives count, and why every last girl has the right to go to school.

The Numbers

I opened my eyes to find women before me, their clothing a dazzling sweep of every shade on an artist's palette—some veiled, some not—every woman wore her red Educate Girls uniform top, uniting everyone in our team colour. As they moved in front of me, I became dizzy. I had approached the microphone but instead grabbed the stand to steady myself as I looked out across the marquee. Some of the women held babies, others bounced toddlers on their knees. And to my left, row upon row of men standing in pale shirts or white kurtas, bright pink and orange turbans dotted the crowd and, again, everyone wore a crimson sweater. I admit my eyesight is not what it used to be, but as I looked out, with balloons adorning every tent pole and the arched ceiling of the enormous tent stretching out like an endless tunnel in front of me, I couldn't even see the last row of seats despite my elevation on the stage. I took a moment to breathe. This was our fifteenth foundation day celebration event, and Meena had called me up on stage to open the proceedings. As I paused, I realized the enormity of the moment. This was a large part of our 22,000-strong team. Here, in one place, were at least 2,000 Team Balika and Educate Girls field staff. Where once the whole team had fitted in one marquee, we were now spread across four states of India. The crowd in front of me had many of our founding team members, girls and volunteers, but this was only a part of what we had become.

'Namaste to you all!' I began. 'I warmly welcome all our friends who have come from the villages of Jalore, Sirohi and Pali. Your presence here is so important to today's celebrations. Do you all know what your hard work has achieved? Your hard work has brought about a change, and it's not a small change but a significant social change that has come about due to connecting millions of girls with education. This is not just a statistic, not just numbers. This is a wave of change that will change the future of all our girls forever!'

I paused and looked out again over the crowd. I could hardly believe how far we had come. The work started here in Pali, and fifteen years later had reached over 30,000 villages across four states of India. We had knocked on around 14 million doors and this incredible effort was all led by our Team Balika and highly dedicated field staff. The fact that we now based our planning on machine-learning algorithms also meant that we were knocking on the right doors a lot faster. I mentioned before that after our first decade we had secured the education of 3,45,000 girls. Now, with this accelerated approach in 2024, we were supporting the enrolment of over 4,00,000 girls in a single year! This truly was now a movement! In just a few years, we had found and mobilized over 1.5 million girls who were all now going to school. Previously, they were invisible and forgotten. Something that should have taken us forty-five years without technology had been managed in just five years thanks to our precision-targeting actions and incredible team!

Given we were now celebrating a decade and a half's work, rather than visiting one or two of our annual foundation day events, I had decided on an all-encompassing road trip. That year, I wanted to really reconnect with our teams and our girls, and revisit the protagonists of our incredible stories. I wanted to try and meet as many girls as possible, see them face to face and reassure myself that all the incredible numbers and stories were real! Over the years, I had stored up story after story in my memory and shared a great many with our supporters across the world. My plan was to travel through Rajasthan and then continue on to Madhya Pradesh and Uttar Pradesh (UP) and see what had changed in the girls' lives and communities through education. In Rajasthan, from Pali we made our way to Rajsamand, Udaipur and then Jhalawar and Barwani. We then crossed over into Madhya Pradesh, visiting Alirajpur, Jhabua, Dhar and Barwani. After that we moved on to Uttar Pradesh, with Prayagraj, Chitrakoot to Robertsgunj and then Fatehpur, Bhairaich and Maharajganj, ending in Siddhi. We attended events that ranged from 800 attendees right up to 2,000. There were men, women, children, media, government officials, donors and supporters, who flew in from far and wide. We also went to revisit some of our closest friends like Vibha and Andu and many others.

It was the time of year when the evenings were cooler. Unlike Mumbai, where the temperatures bounce 10 degrees or so from season to season, in Rajasthan, Madhya Pradesh and Uttar Pradesh the difference can be more like 20 degrees between summer and winter. As we drove through the districts of Pali, Rajasamund, Udaipur and Jhalawar, there were constant changes in the landscape with brutal, dry plains rising into hills and back down again. The population is very sparse except when people are crowded into a fourteen-seater jeep, and we regularly saw thirty to forty people crammed into one vehicle. The odd town suddenly appeared and disappeared again and we knew we were in Rajasthan by the colourful turbans worn by the men.

When we reached Banswara—Andu's community—on the border with Madhya Pradesh, and crossed into Jhabua and Dhar, we met with deep forests. The road narrowed from

12 to 10 feet and it seemed to me that the colour of attire faded too. Uttar Pradesh was another sharp contrast, and despite its size and diversity, was obviously a lot more densely populated. One village ran straight into the next, with no pause, no space. The roads were crammed with two-wheelers—far more so than in Rajasthan and Madhya Pradesh—and a 200-kilometre journey took almost twice as long because of the traffic. We learnt the hard way and Google Maps was no help at all. We covered over 4,500 kilometres with our patient driver, and visited all sixteen districts, celebrating the anniversary of Educate Girls since it was formally registered back in December 2007. In every district, we had similar experiences and people came from, really far, places.

On one occasion 800 people descended on a village and there was nowhere to stay. They had been invited for the Monday early morning meeting, but on Sunday night word had spread and additional groups of people arrived on foot and by the busload, some on the back of mopeds, as if the village was hosting a festival. Vikram called me in a panic about the need to find accommodation for everyone. It was winter. It was cold. But the panic subsided as the team pulled together. They searched the length and breadth of the village and ensured we took every room in every hotel and dharamshalas attached to the temples. Rooms that were meant for four people became dorms for six or eight. Our staff stayed up all night, bought bottled water and snacks and made sure that everyone was looked after. We truly had not anticipated that this many young people, with their parents in many cases, would arrive to celebrate fifteen years of working for girls' education.

One near catastrophe was when a team member inadvertently disturbed a hive of bees right next to an event in progress. A dark, humming cloud moved menacingly towards our marquee, where already 1,000 women, men and children were gathered. Can you imagine what might have happened if the bees had entered and become trapped in the tent? Vikram and a few field officers rushed to seal the marquee. With a sigh of relief, knowing that everyone was now safe, they approached me looking shocked but pleased with their quick thinking. But of course, halfway through sharing their story with me, they realized that I was on the wrong side of that tent wall. The crowd inside were waiting to hear from me as it was me who was going to open the whole event! How glamorous I felt as I got on my hands and knees in my beautifully ironed saree and squeezed under the side of the tent, emerging from under the stage dishevelled, to the surprise of all, while another set of team members valiantly continued to calm the bees. My dignity remained intact, unlike the time I was followed by a drone as I made my 'grand' entrance to one of the events, and ended up tripping up the step and falling flat! There was also the time once when the stage caught on fire.

Over the two months of events held across sixteen districts, 11,928 volunteers and 2,765 staff members were present at the gatherings. All our longest-standing team members joined us, and some members like Vikram also hit the road with me to ensure his presence at every event. As I write, with that image of the crowds in my mind, I find it hard to comprehend how we went from meeting a handful of individuals back in 2007 to having close to 22,000 people standing with us, giving their time in the hope of finding and educating every last girl.

This was the first time the enormity of our work really struck me, but this really wasn't just about the numbers. As I stood there looking at the eyes staring up at me, I wondered to myself what girls' education meant to everyone standing before me. I knew what it meant to me. I was here today because of my education. In the front row with Meena and Vikram, I saw Andu. Her education meant that she had saved her daughter's life, who had grown up to pass her Class 10 exams and was then studying for Class 11. The cycle had been broken, her life had changed. Vibha caught my eye with a warm smile, and I thought about her studies, what her education meant to her. She was now working and supporting her sister to return to education. All these women and girls were now able to write their own stories, and my trip was about the stories, much more than just the numbers.

Beyond the Numbers

Every single girl in that marquee, in all those villages we traversed, was an individual with a life of her own. Every one of those 1.5 million girls across all our state programmes had a name, an identity and now the prospect of an education. Each girl was a daughter, a sister and a future mother, if she so chose. Each girl might be a teacher, a healthcare worker, an entrepreneur or a politician. Education meant something different to each girl; most importantly, every girl's story began with her right and her freedom to have a voice and to choose her own path.

With a decade and a half between our early days and the organization we are today, I never get complacent. The perils of illiteracy and the lack of a quality education cannot be forgotten. But we are now able to tell the stories of how education is overcoming those perils and how change really is happening, one girl at a time and one village at a time.

Remember Jassi's mother whose bank ripped her off when she tried to withdraw her hard-earned savings? We now hear so many accounts of how being able to read helps women avoid such exploitation and fraud. It was widely publicized how the Prime Minister's Swachh Bharat Abhiyan scheme worked with an explicit goal of making India 'open defecation free'. By 2019, over 100 million individual toilets had been constructed in people's homes, across the length and breadth of the country. The scheme involved a 12,000-rupee contribution and technical assistance provided to citizens. But when one such Swachh Bharat official came to Sapna's village, he was asking for a fee to help her family access the scheme. Sapna retorted with a firm 'no'. She knew. She had seen the posters, she had read and understood the pamphlet. Sapna was educated and was not going to be ripped off! As I sat with Sapna and her friends on one of my village visits, indignant stories came tumbling out. Almost all of them could cite a story of attempted fraud, and of how being able to read had empowered them to stand up to exploitation, know their rights and use their knowledge to push back against everything from online theft to deception in access to government schemes!

Illiteracy really can be a matter of safety, even life or death. Stories that we use in our village meetings to illustrate the perils of illiteracy, like the story of the eye ointment and the tyre glue mix-up, are not just stories, they are a harsh reality, and the meaning of education in a medical situation is plain to see. Samitha explained to me how her sister had fallen on the ground a few months back and suffered a terrible seizure. Samitha's illiterate mother was hell-bent on taking her to the village healer. But Samitha insisted on rushing her to a registered medical facility in the nearby town. She was not going to wait for her father or brother. Samitha ran to the local rickshaw driver and she and her sister, Varsha, made the rapid journey unaccompanied. Varsha made a full recovery, but the doctors explained to the two girls that she had been very lucky and it was Samhita's quick thinking and insistence on seeking proper medical advice immediately that meant that she survived. Epilepsy often goes undiagnosed in rural India. Access to pretenders and local, unqualified healers is often easier than seeking proper medical assistance. Folklore and ideas passed down through families and communities can often mean that advances in medicine don't reach villages. Knowledge gained in school and the confidence to enter a medical facility were critical in Samhita's life-saving actions. But it is still quite shocking to learn that as recently as 2017 close to 80 per cent of women in India still had to ask a male family member's permission to visit a health centre.[1]

Land and property ownership can be a complex undertaking—remember Poonam, whose nephew stole her land in the weeks following her husband's sudden death? Grief, misplaced trust and an inability to read forced Poonam to sign away what was rightfully hers. But on the other hand, there is Vijaya, one of the girls we enrolled in Pali. She joined me one afternoon to fill me in on what she was now up to. Recently, she had done all the paperwork for her aunt's purchase of a flat, cutting out the need for a broker, saving 20,000 rupees, earning herself a small fee by way of a thank-you and giving her invaluable experience in conveyancing and understanding property contracts. Vijaya exuded modest pride as she recounted her story, and she really deserves to be proud because studies show that 48 per cent of young women in India are not allowed to make decisions about buying land or property, 44 per cent are not even allowed to decide to buy a household item like a fridge![2] Vijaya now lives alone, is working, earning, riding a motorbike and plans to save up for her own place. Her education has given her freedom she might never have had. Losing both parents at a young age might have thrown her out of school and into the grip of a child marriage. But when we enrolled her in school, Vijaya thrived and her education has certainly given her the skills to negotiate contracts and embark on a path to home ownership for herself one day.

As Vijaya pulled her helmet over her short, cropped hair and straddled her motorbike, the symbolism was so clear to me. Education was bringing a mobility these girls had never before seen in their villages. School opened up a world beyond the village, school trips included visits to incredible historic sites—forts, temples, resorts. But this mobility also meant an ability to live independently.

'Because you are educated you can travel alone!' was what Jyoti was told by her mother, when she had saved up enough money to visit her brother in Pune, Maharashtra. She might have assumed she would need a chaperone. But this was no longer the case. The family had saved up and Jyoti navigated buying her ticket, travelling to the airport and flying to Pune, alone. A stark contrast to older family members, whose illiteracy meant they couldn't even read the number on the local bus without help. Our recruitment of young women was hampered by traditional mindsets that suggested women couldn't move around unaccompanied, couldn't undertake the kind of work we were asking of them. Jyoti was the symbol of change.

What does being able to drive mean? To a girl, working hard in a farming family it means being able to drive a tractor, fast-tracking days of hard labour, being able to transport irrigation equipment to the farm and saving crops in today's unpredictable waves of heat. Collecting water can take a girl up to four hours a day. Where is the time to read, to study, to go to school? With the time freed up, she can study and meet friends, and some of her time can become her own. This mobility changes a lot.

Female Leadership

Aarohi was in the front row at one of our foundation day event and she joined me on stage to share stories about her education and her local leadership. She was now used to addressing crowds, having served for six years as the sarpanch for seven villages in her locality. We hadn't met her for a number of years, but one day in 2022 when we were back in Falna we heard a cry across a village junction: 'Vijayalakshmi-ji, what are you doing here?'

We halted in our tracks, narrowly avoiding a two-wheeler as it turned the corner. As we looked back over our shoulders, we saw a slim lady emerge from a shop. She wore a red saree, her head covered just behind neatly parted hair and a darker red bindi between her excited-looking eyes. In one hand she carried a plastic bag and waved furiously with the other to draw our attention.

Our morning had started early with a Team Balika meeting in Falna. They had travelled far from villages in the block and we had held a very moving meeting, hearing incredible stories from all the volunteers about how things were going now the schools were about to reopen after the pandemic. Vijayalakshmi and I had left the hotel, where we had hosted the team and were now crossing a busy intersection. Three black and yellow rickshaws were lined up, one of the driver's feet protruding from where he would usually be sitting as he took his afternoon siesta. The other two drivers leant up against their vehicles smoking bidis and engaged in an animated conversation. We spotted a cart across the road that sold sugarcane juice, partly obscured by the rickshaws. I persuaded Vijayalakshmi to come with me for a quick drink. Just as we tentatively put a foot out on the road, we heard a cry behind us from a store we had just passed.

'*Main Aarohi hoon*! Vijayalakshmi-ji, you enrolled me in school back in 2010! Remember me?' she hollered. She trotted down the road to greet us! Others who were busy looking in the stores, going about their business, paused to watch us approach one another.

Aarohi must have been about twenty-three years old but the energy she exuded was of someone much younger. We decided to all cross the street and pull up on a bench by the sugarcane juice vendor. Vijayalakshmi placed our order, and we settled into a conversation as we sipped on our sweet refreshments. Aarohi and Vijayalakshmi reacquainted themselves. There were a lot of affirmations and agreements as they reminded each other of all that had passed over the decade since they had been in touch. Vijayalakshmi and the team had enrolled Aarohi in school when the office in Falna had been around for a couple of years and we were slowly expanding the team. Aarohi filled me in on her story.

Having nearly missed out on an education, Aarohi's enrolment in her local KGBV had all been down to Vijayalakshmi. She was one of five children, and when her alcoholic father died, Aarohi truly felt that education was not going to be possible for her. Looking back now, her education meant so much to her that as soon as she was in a leadership position in the panchayat of seven villages, she allocated a majority of her administrative budget to education and, specifically, girls' education. Like in Andu's villages, girls' education meant a transformation in this area too. Girls now accessed their rights to freedom of movement, to freedom of speech, to marry at adulthood, to work, to rest, to get an education and to live with one another as equals.

Meeting Aarohi again was one of those incredible happenstances. There is no getting away from the fact that we can sometimes get lost in our data and numbers. But when we learn of a journey that started with a Team Balika member enrolling a girl in school, and then ten years later we witness her address a crowd of thousands and explain how she used her education for the education of other girls, we know that what we are doing is working!

A New Normal

As I dug into the meaning of each girl's education, a pattern of change started to emerge, and when we look at this in the context of generational change we start to see the evolution of a new normal. A new normal that each girl provides a new precedent and a new role model. And this in turn empowers the next girl, and then the next, to stay in school.

One little girl I was taken to meet recently was Ganaki. She was the youngest of five daughters. Pyari, Rupa, Gomati and Hansi were all born to Savli Devi, and a few years later, she (finally) had a son Ratan. We first met Savli Devi when she should really have been sending her girls to school. But Pyari had never been to school and Rupa had just completed Class 8 and had been at home since. When it came to the other three girls, the decision was difficult. Now life was tough and although she believed in education, Savli Devi was struggling—having lost her husband—and when we met her, none of her three younger girls were going to school. They had completed their fifth grade but she was hesitant to let them complete any more years of schooling. Despite the RTE, the village school only went up to Class 5. The next phase of education was going to be a challenge. It was just at this stage that Bablu, part of Team Balika, started working in their village and he persuaded Savli Devi that having Rupa and Pyari at home to help with her baby boy and the farm was enough. It was really important for the other three girls to continue at least to eighth grade at the KGBV. So the three girls, who had gotten rather used to their work in the fields, went back to school. Gomati and Hansi had to catch up on a year or so of being out of school. Ganaki managed the transition without a break.

Without Rupa as an example, I do wonder if these vibrant young ladies would have received the education they did.

Perhaps she was the first role model that started a pattern. I do wonder what had changed between Pyari, who stayed at home and never enrolled, and Rupa, who managed to stay in school until eighth grade. Savli put it down to the fact that Pyari was naughty and kept running away from school. Was she naughty or was that a time when children, particularly girls, from lower-caste families would often be ridiculed in class? Corporal punishment was still rife. School was a very different place back then. Our teams knew this family well, but there are sometimes mysteries we can't always get to the bottom of, particularly over the period of a decade.

But with each child gaining a little more education the path was forged for the next child to gain even more. Another girl we met in the same village, a friend of Ganaki's, was one of ten children. She described her siblings to me from the first to the last—each child gained a little more education than the last over the decade. From her eldest sister who never went to school, to her next sister who gained three years of education, a few siblings who dropped out at fifth or eighth, and finally to Paru, who was a 'twelfth-pass'. Here was a family who had spanned the decade and a half since the RTE Act and demonstrated incremental change.

Savli Devi crouched at the entrance to the small room on one side of the courtyard of their home where we sat. As the light streamed in, it caught the edge of her glasses and exposed the evidence of a relatively recent cataract operation. Gomati played around with her toddler, constantly adjusting her veil and glued to her mobile phone. Meanwhile, Ganaki and Hansi sat with us and talked extensively about their lives.

Their education meant that the two girls had shaken off a lot of the community's expectations. Where Gomati looked very much the traditional married young woman in her red saree and shiny toe rings and bangles, Hansi and Ganaki sat comfortably in their jeans. Ganaki sported a pair of wire-framed glasses and a maroon kurta; Hansi wore a short-sleeved navy blue T-shirt with Mickey Mouse emblazoned on it. They laughed and passed around a smartphone and busily responded to our discussions on what one needed to travel to the UK, searching how much might an air ticket cost and details about the visa. Behind the girls at the back of the room was a long, coiled-up irrigation hose. The girls no longer needed to carry heavy water urns on their heads back from the well. When they needed to irrigate their family fields, they jumped on a motorbike and took the hose to the water tap and the fields were promptly watered. Like Vijaya and Anisha, Ganaki had a driving licence and wheels. She had the kind of mobility that was unheard of when her older sister was her age. She explained all this with an energy and infectious confidence.

As we walked through the village together, we spotted a couple of tractors and their size surprised me as I recalled how Ganaki had just told me that not only could she get to her fields faster on her bike, but she could also drive a tractor when needed to till the ground or help with the harvest!

There is still an obvious clash of progress with tradition in this household. While the girls pursue their BAs, they are still committed to marry next year in April on Akshaya Tritiya, an auspicious date considered lucky for a wedding or starting a business. In the past, a large number of child marriages would take place on this date. It is costly to find an individual auspicious date for weddings so an economical way of doing it is to marry when other community members marry too. Ganaki and Hansi will marry on the same day. It's an economic decision.

We quizzed the girls on their ability to access more information in the pursuit of better farming practices. They agreed that this was certainly the case. A year or so ago they got a soil test card and the girls interpreted the card and guidance correctly, leading to an understanding that their soil had enough nitrogen and was lacking other nutrients. An overuse of widely available urea had rendered their soil infertile. A little bit of research and understanding the results of the soil test card enabled the family to switch to gypsum on their fields instead. Steadily, over a couple of harvests, the soil and yield had improved. None of this would have been possible without their education.

But relying on weather updates from their phones didn't always help. Each farm is linked to the next—you can only reach your own field when your neighbours plough theirs first. The work is interdependent, tied to the rhythm of the community and its traditions. So even when someone has new information, they can't always act on it if those around them continue with age-old practices. Just last year the girls had planted their seeds at 'the usual time' but heavy rains flooded the field, water stood still on the land for a long time and destroyed the seeds. The girls were just not able to stand up to the elders and change their ways. Everyone had to work together. And there was a resigned acceptance by the girls of their elder's rules and their compliant, impending marriage.

'For my mother's sake, I just don't want people to think I am a *buree ladki* [bad girl],' Ganaki explained in a solemn tone.

What I haven't yet told you is the meaning of Ganaki's name. Savli Devi started off her family with Pyari (precious), Rupa (blessed), Gomati (river) and then Hansi (pure). Her much-awaited son's name meant 'treasure'. But after four girls, awaiting and wishing for a baby boy, Savli Devi named her fifth daughter Ganaki, which means 'enough'. We had also counted and documented in our door-to-door survey girls whose name meant 'stop', 'fed up', 'sorry' or 'the last girl'.—and then I found myself sitting in front of the most energetic, intelligent and wise young girl called 'Enough'.

We left the village feeling that Ganaki was an inspirational young woman. She was making sure that she had education, mobility and knowledge. As she left her veil at home and looked out on the world, she perhaps had more choice, the voice to delay her marriage, complete her studies and perhaps fulfil her dreams. Evidence supports the fact that she will be healthier, maybe happier; she will educate her children, stand up to discrimination and abuse and, we hope, become a leader and role model for others. Completing fifth grade was not enough, nor eighth or tenth. Even a twelfth-pass qualification was not enough education for this strident young woman. Ganaki's BA and potentially MA will set a precedent for other girls in her village and perhaps she will turn the page on a better future for herself and her friends and neighbours, for many more girls, and perhaps even every last girl.

Conclusion

The Path Ahead

Eighteen years ago, I started Educate Girls out of a pistachio-coloured house in a quiet residential area near Falna, Rajasthan. Today, we have expanded to four states, with multiple offices and plans to reach seven more states in the next five years. Over these years, we have entered 30,000 villages—areas with the most critical gender gaps in education. There, along with the local leaders—our army of gender champions, Team Balika—we have changed mindsets and brought over two million girls back into the classroom, where they belong.

And yet, while telling this story, I have left out something vital: the quality of the education received by our girls and their fellow male students, once they enrol.

It is a question we face all the time: what is the point of enrolling a girl into school if what she then learns is irrelevant, unengaging and of poor quality? It is a fair question. The truth is, we have worked just as hard to ensure that the curriculum and teaching practices inside the classroom are as transformative as the journey was to get there. Working alongside government teachers and experts in pedagogy and special education, we have created a 'repository of learning'—*Gyan ka Pitara*—that has helped our Team Balika and field staff ensure that children are engaged in learning, stay in school, move to the next grade, pass their exams, learn to read and learn to learn. This, in turn, is evidenced by academics and researchers, who carry out gold-standard external audits and evaluations to ensure our classroom interventions are effective.

The results speak for themselves. We have a measurable positive impact on foundational literacy and numeracy for children, who are very often first-generation learners. Through rigorous evaluation, including randomized control trials—similar to those used in the healthcare sector—we have seen out-of-school girl numbers drop dramatically, with more girls entering classrooms. Children in third, fourth and fifth grade are gaining the equivalent of an additional year of learning—an extra year they would previously have missed out on. They are staying in school and developing vital life skills.

We have also tracked our work with young boys. They, too, have been counted and enrolled. They sit in the same classrooms and benefit from the improved teaching tools, as well as from growing up in communities, where the value of education is more widely understood.

Our numbers are large and our evidence is strong. But I keep coming back to the stories. More than anything, this journey has taught us profound lessons about out-of-school girls: who they are, where they are, what holds them back and how we can help bring them into school—sometimes for the very first time.

We have discovered that most out-of-school girls live on the margins—in remote villages, in poor households, from lower castes and, owing to the near-universal preference for sons, surrounded by gender bias in every aspect of life. We have learned how to identify 'hot spots', where the numbers of vulnerable girls are disproportionately high. We have learned how to shift mindsets in such communities by building teams of hyper-local village-based champions—who ultimately become our Team Balika volunteers.

We now understand that mindset change does not happen when you tell people what they *should* be doing. It does not happen with presenting data and statistics. Those numbers may guide us, but they mean little to the girls or their families. Nor does change happen through information overload, or when you parachute in from elsewhere to deliver a message. Real change comes from the right messenger. In our case, that messenger is a Team Balika volunteer: someone driven by purpose, from the village and of the village.

We discovered this early on, but over the years we have refined our approach. Today we can say with confidence that the key ingredient for mindset change is authentic storytelling—stories that show the real impact of education in people's lives. It is not about slick brochures or polished PowerPoint slides. It is about hearing from a human being who comes from that village, who understands their context and struggles. When a compassionate community member tells an authentic personal story of transformation, it resonates. Behavioural change comes from that emotional connection, from the ability to see oneself in the storyteller and one's life reflected in the story.

'If you can do it, then maybe I can too. If you can send your girls to school, then maybe I can too.'

We have learned how to scale this solution to thousands of villages, homes and schools. With the use of artificial intelligence—specifically machine learning—we can now predict the number of out-of-school girls in each village and ensure we reach the hardest areas as quickly as possible. And an unintended but powerful consequence of all our work has been the sense of purpose given to 55,000 gender champions across the country.

Did We Find Her?

But our quest is not yet over. Have we found Antimbala? Is it a happy ending? We might have found 233 girls called Antimbala, counted and safely logged in our data systems. Two hundred and thirty-three Antimbalas back in school, amongst the two million others. But did we find *the* Antimbala? Did we find every last girl?

The answer, as I am sure you can guess, is no. In our quest to find Antimbala, we have aligned with the Right to Education Act and focused on elementary education, which includes first to eighth grades, ages six to fourteen. What we have seen, however, is that the older adolescent girls we meet—walking the fields with a baby strapped to their hip, hunched over a wood fire in the corner of their home, scaling the hillside with a herd of goats—face a *much* higher mountain to climb. Whilst elementary education has seen tremendous progress, as girls progress through school the dropout rate in primary years of less than 1 per cent, rises to close to 4 per cent in middle school, and balloons up when they reach secondary school. So much so that close to 40 per cent of girls in India are destined not to complete the 10th grade.[1] What does this mean in the life of a girl?

I had my own education story to look back on—the hurdles I had to overcome. I managed to avoid an early marriage and return to school, yet I had little idea how being excluded from the 10th grade impacted girls until I met Pooja.

Pooja is a nineteen-year-old I met in a village in Jodhpur district during a field visit in mid-2024. When I asked her name, she immediately looked down, her eyes filling with tears. It took a lot of courage for her even to tell me, her first utterance so quiet that I had to ask her to repeat it. Slowly, she opened up. She told me how she had wanted to study but could not. She got married very young and moved away from her home district to live with her in-laws. With great difficulty, she explained it was not a good marriage. Her husband was abusive, and her in-laws blamed her for his alcoholism and violence. Eventually, she could not bear it any longer and returned to live with her parents.

Pooja had dropped out of school in ninth grade because of her marriage. She would have been fifteen then. Now she wakes at 3 a.m. every day and goes to the vegetable market, where she unloads delivery trucks—sacks of onions, baskets of leafy vegetables and herbs, all hoisted down from looming vehicles. It is good that she is tall, for it is back-breaking work. The trucks arrive before sunrise, and it is Pooja's job to deliver the produce to the shops, back and forth in the near-dark. By 8 a.m. she returns home to cook, clean and fetch water. By early evening, she is back at the market again, cleaning shops and sweeping the pavements, strewn with onion peelings and trodden coriander leaves from the day's trade.

Once the market closes, she returns home to do more chores before collapsing to sleep. After barely a few hours' rest, it is 3 a.m. again and the cycle begins anew. Exhaustion and resignation coloured her voice as she told me her story. '*Yeh meri zindagi hai …*' she said. 'This is my life, from today till the day I die.' She had no hope that anything would change. Pooja desperately wants to go back to education. She longs to study more, but with the gap in her schooling, she is no longer eligible for the formal education system. Her only option is distance education through the National Institute of Open Schooling. But enrolment and exam centres are only in urban and peri-urban areas. For a girl like Pooja, for whom the nearest town is a costly bus ride away, it is simply too expensive. It would cost thousands of rupees to enrol—money she does not have, and that neither her parents nor her in-laws will pay.

If Pooja could complete her tenth grade credential—the equivalent of a high school diploma—the world would begin to open up. This qualification is the bare minimum for an entry-level job, the minimum requirement to register for 60–70 per cent of skill and vocational courses and, in some places, even the minimum to secure a formal bank loan. Despite all the progress made, together with the government's mandate on elementary education, a huge barrier remains for girls who reach eighth grade but can go no further. It leaves them just short of life opportunities. Eight years of education is of course a gain, but it is not enough to open the doors to a better life.

Through Pooja's story, I was beginning to see why 81 per cent of women in India remain unskilled and why only 42 per cent are in the labour force.[2] India lacks secondary schools on a massive scale. For every hundred primary schools, we have only twenty secondary schools.[3] In the early 2000s, the primary challenge was mindset and aspiration. At the secondary level, it is infrastructure. The schools simply do not exist in sufficient numbers for girls living in poverty. Even if families want to send them, they cannot.

Back before the Right to Education Act, there was reluctance—an absence of ambition that every child could or should go to school. The number of out-of-school children seemed daunting, even insurmountable. But with the government's will and grassroots efforts, a generation was moved into classrooms. I hear echoes of that old reluctance again. People say: 'Well, we can't build secondary schools for all. She should just join tailoring or some skill course. Perhaps she can join a self-help group and get a loan to start a business. Since there are barely enough jobs for men, she should forget about studies and employment. Where are the jobs anyway?'

But what if she *wants* to study? Perhaps for dignity or self-respect in the community. Perhaps she sees education as a pathway to opportunity—or perhaps she simply wants it for herself. Too often society at large, and even the well-meaning social development community, is at fault. Everyone thinks they know what is best for her. Everyone wants to dictate how much is enough. We decide what a girl should settle for. We have opinions on what she should do, wear, say or aspire to—just as others decide where she can go, who she can meet or marry. All too often, her story is written for her. But this is not right, and it is not what I am prepared to settle for. I always centre on what *she* wants. If she wants to study, then that is what we as a society must provide, whatever her reason. Yet again, I remain resolved in my understanding that education is not something for us to give or take away as we see fit. It is not a gift. It is every girl's right—no matter her age or what she plans to do with the education and her life.

The Next Mountain

Pooja, and millions of girls like her, cannot go back to formal schools. They are overage, have experienced long gaps in their schooling or have failed an exam that has closed the door on further learning. It is now up to us to find a way to move their educational journey forward. Educate Girls has always been a story about girls and the government. Fortunately, there is already a government policy to guide the next phase of our work. India's National Education Policy, 2020, covers the needs of such girls—at least in theory—with the bold ambition to ensure that girls and young women can access education beyond the traditional system. At the heart of this policy is a plan to strengthen the open school system for every girl who needs it.

We have seen before what a tailwind large policy shifts can provide. The Right to Education Act and Beti Bachao, Beti Padhao were transformative, and once again we must work hand in hand with the government to activate this policy so that it reaches girls like Pooja. But here is where we all come in. We cannot allow 50 per cent of India's girls, who have failed to make it to secondary school or dropped out along the way, to be denied a second chance. This is the next mountain Educate Girls must climb. It is a steep one. Millions of girls want to study but cannot, because of the limitations of our current education system. They need another chance.

And that is my dream. After eighteen years in this field, I know it is a dream that can become a reality—we know how to do this, and we have the skills and the movement to make it happen. Our network of gender champions, the backbone of our organization, are also a web of activists already working with communities and state governments across the country to turn this vision into reality.

Educate Girls now has a bold goal: to change the lives of ten million more learners in the next ten years. But this time, our focus will include older girls—those like Pooja, whose first chance was cut short, but whose second chance is within reach if we support them. If the central and state governments create lifelong learning platforms for all girls, we will finally have a safety net to catch those who have dropped out of formal schooling or never made it there at all.

That is the role of the government. But the lack of girls' education and the persistence of gender inequality, are also societal problems. So what is it that we—the people—must do? First, we must be aware of the issue and its urgency. India's invisible daughters must be made visible. Second, we must actively support the very idea of girls' education, wherever and however we can. That means being mindful of the conscious and unconscious biases we carry, and ensuring we do not replicate them within our own families and communities.

Imagine if India woke up tomorrow and believed, truly believed, that our sons and daughters are equal. We would not need Educate Girls. We would not have this problem of gender bias. In a single sweep, we would have a society that believes in equality. No extraordinary interventions would be required. The problem lies in our minds, so we must confront our learned biases—and unlearn them, quickly—before another generation of girls miss out on education, opportunity and self-respect.

While the government can and must meet its obligation to provide an education for every child, the deeper responsibility rests with us all.

A Dream

I had been piecing this book together for over a year. While I made progress, it was hard to write and reflect whilst keeping up with the day-to-day demands of running an organization and a family. Zoom meetings, travel, decisions, events. The urgent always trumped what was important—and for me, writing down this story was important. Yet it was constantly sidelined by the daily grind. So I applied for the Rockefeller Foundation's Bellagio Residency in Lombardy, Italy. The programme runs for a month and, as an aspiring writer, a leader, a 'traveller' on a professional journey, you are invited to step away from everyday work and live full-time at the centre on the banks of Lake Como in northern Italy.

The Bellagio Centre is utterly beautiful, awe-inspiring—especially in April, when the soft spring sun warms the gardens, flowers bloom everywhere and the scent of wisteria follows you through the grounds. From my room, the view of the lake was like a painting. Below the centre, lay the stunning little town, glamorous motorboats skimming across the water day and night.

And yet, in the midst of all this backdrop of beauty and quiet, I was not sleeping. My mind was not quiet. Not only was I not sleeping—I was having intense, vivid nightmares almost every night. I would wake up stunned, the visions hanging over me like a bad hangover through the day.

I could not understand it. Why was I so unsettled, so disturbed? After a few nights of struggling, and trying to fight it with sleeping tablets, I decided to surrender to what was happening. Instead of searching for an escape, I thought, let me sit with these dreams. Let me reflect on what they are trying to tell me. 'Calmly, without fear or anxiety, face the dreams,' I told myself.

The very next night, after making this decision, the dreams became worse. I woke at 2:30 a.m., clammy and drenched in sweat, as if I were back in rural Rajasthan on a hot May afternoon. Sleep refused to return. After hours of tossing and turning, I gave in, opened my laptop, and began working through emails, hoping the tether to the outside world might still my racing mind.

By 4:30 or 5 a.m., when I finally returned to bed, I had one of the most frightening dreams of all. I was inside a vast construction site—unfinished walls, concrete beams, staircases half-built, no roof. I was trying to escape, to navigate these perilous stairs without rails or balustrades, with sheer darkness yawning below. It felt like an Escher painting, a maze of danger. Clutching the side of a wall, I tried to descend but grew dizzy, knowing that one slip would send me plummeting.

I entered a room with a glass window. In the glass, I saw myself—but not a mirror image. Another Safeena. She looked like me, wore her hair the same, but her clothes were different, and she did not copy my movements. Her arms flailed in distress. Though her lips moved, I could hear no sound. Still, I understood: she was asking me to help her. She pointed desperately to a section of the wall beneath the glass, urging me to break it so she could escape.

They say that in dreams one should focus less on the characters, more on the feelings. And I was afraid. Afraid of what might be released if I let that girl out. What ghosts might come tumbling through the opening? In the dream I found an iron bar and tried to smash the wall. I managed only a small opening. From it poured a thick, foul sludge. It oozed everywhere, suffocating. I was paralyzed—torn between freeing the girl and overwhelmed by the onslaught. I cried for help. The dream had no resolution. I woke gasping for breath.

The next day I sat down to write, to think, to reflect. I was here in Bellagio to write my book about Antimbala—the last girl. This was meant to be my account of a journey across villages to find her. But was my mind was telling me something different? Was my quest really about Antimbala or had it always been about the little Safeena?

I had always thought of my work with Educate Girls as strategic, data-driven and evidence-based. It is all that—but it is also more. It is about the little girl inside me. The Safeena trapped at thirteen years old, longing to escape poverty, violence and abuse. The Safeena carrying shame and failure, hypervigilant, anxious and always waiting for something bad to happen.

Perhaps my dreams are reminding me that this work is not only an outward search but also an inward one—the work of healing her wounds, meeting her needs. The journey continues until that little girl finds peace.

She is my last girl. She is my Antimbala.

I am Safeena Husain, and I educate girls.

Their Names, Their Stories

Aachuki (arrived): Third daughter of Sitaram and Pooja Devi, from Sirohi. Dropped out of school after 3 years to work in the fields. Enrolled into grade 5, by Swati, her Team Balika in 2017.

Nakushi (unwanted): Only daughter of Jagdish and Sita, from Jalore. Never went to school. Enrolled into grade 1, two years late, by Hemant, her Team Balika in 2012.

Faltu (useless): Fourth daughter of Sogoram and Kamla Devi, from Pali. Dropped out of school after a year. Enrolled into grade 2 by Ramlal, in 2012.

Manbhaari (heavy heart): Third daughter of Ranjit and Mansor, from Rajsamand. Never went to school as she looked after her baby brother. Enrolled into year 1, when 7 years old, by Pooja, her Team Balika, in 2015.

Maafi (sorry): Third daughter of Jitendra and Pinta Devi, from Jhalawar. Dropped out aged 12 after a prolonged fever. Enrolled into grade 6 by Sanjay, her Team Balika, in 2013.

Dhaapu (fed up): Second daughter of Dunga Ram and Gomti Devi, from Udaipur district. Dropped out after grade

8 after Dunga Ram passed away. Enrolled into grade 9 aged 16, by her team Balika Swati in 2019.

Naraaz (angry): Fifth daughter of Babu and Dubli, from Salumber. Never went to school. Enrolled into grade 2 by her Team Balika Kuldeep in 2010

Galla (stop): Third daughter of Bharat and Lila, from Banswara. Dropped out of school after grade 5 when her Mother had to move to Udaipur for work. Enrolled by Rinku, her Team Balika in 2017.

Antimbala (last one): Fourth daughter of Mansingh and Kavita, from Jhabua. Never went to school. Enrolled by Farzana, her Team Balika in 2020.

This book is dedicated to every one of these girls, and every last girl who has been denied an education. Whether she has made it into the classroom or remains excluded from a future that should be hers. She might be walking the ASALs in Kenya, crook in hand, goats at her feet. She might be in the Swat Valley, cooking over a wood burning stove. She might have been kidnapped from a school in a village in Nigeria or hiding from the Taliban in Helmand Province. She might be in Rajasthan, Bihar or Odisha in India. Wherever she is, this book is for her.

Acknowledgements

I would first of all like to thank my mother, Usha, and my aunt, Mahe. Without them this story would never have begun. My patient family who stood by me not only through the writing of this book, but through the whole Educate Girls journey: Hansal, Jai, Pallav, Kimaya and Rihanna, thank you.

To the whole team at Educate Girls, many of whom feature in the book and others who have been instrumental in its research and writing: Vikram, Meena, Jassi, Vijayalakshmi, Ramlal, Farzana, Kuldeep, Brajesh, Akhil, Shovik, Payal, Shwetha, Ashwini, Abjy, Abigail, Bineesh, Shabnam, Maharshi, Viji and Sharanya—this is *our* story and I am incredibly grateful that you have helped me in sharing it with the world. Publishing a book is a first for us, and I'm deeply thankful for the guidance from the publishing team at HarperCollins India. Isha, you have been a great support, and I would also like to thank Aashim Raj, Shreya Chakravertty and Shreya Mukherjee for all their hard work. This book would not exist without the guidance and support of Kanishka, my superstar agent, and my most special thanks goes to Alison Bukhari, my rock through thick and thin, whose dedicated support made it possible for me to even attempt this project.

My time with the Rockefeller Foundation in Bellagio was truly inspirational in finalizing the book. I'd like to thank the whole April 2025 cohort and, in particular, Rahul, Sushmita, Carl and Lorenna, for reading over chapters and being a sounding board. To the partners and supporters of Educate Girls: you provide the fuel for this mission and unlock dreams for millions of girls, you know who you are and you too are part of this book.

The Educate Girls story began with my loving father and biggest cheerleader, Yusuf Husain. He lives on in my every breath and the story does not end here …

Notes

Preface

1. UNESCO is the leading global authority on data related to out-of-school children. In 2022, it reported that India ranks among the top five countries with the highest number of such children. 'New measurement shows that 244 million children and youth are out of school', UNESCO, 1 September 2022. https://world-education-blog.org/2022/09/01/new-measurement-shows-that-244-million-children-and-youth-are-out-of-school/. Accessed 5 October 2025. For more details on out-of-school children, see: 'Out-of-School Rate', UNESCO Institute for Statistics. https://education-estimates.org/out-of-school/. Accessed on 5 October 2025.
   Also, the female literacy rate, according to the 2019–21 National Family Health Survey-5 (NFHS-5), is 71.5 per cent. NFHS-5 defines female literacy as the percentage of women (ages 15–49) who have completed at least class 9 or who are able to read a whole sentence or part of a sentence. See: International Institute for Population Sciences (IIPS) and ICF. 'National Family Health Survey (NFHS-5), 2019–21: India, Vol. 1', IIPS, 2021. https://dhsprogram.com/pubs/pdf/FR375/FR375.pdf.
2. Angela Glover Blackwell, 'The Curb-Cut Effect', *Stanford Social Innovation Review*, https://ssir.org/articles/entry/the_curb_cut_effect. As Blackwell wrote: 'An economist might call it a "positive externality". A military officer might call it a "force

multiplier". I like to think of it as the "curb-cut effect"—and it's changing the way the country thinks about the struggles of the most vulnerable communities.'

Introduction

1. A. Firth Murray, *From Outrage to Courage: Women Taking Action for Health and Justice* (Monroe, ME, 2008), p. xiii.
2. Hillary Rodham Clinton, 'Women's Rights Are Human Rights', Speech, United Nations Fourth World Conference on Women, Beijing, China, 5 September 1995, https://www.clintonlibrary.gov/museum/first-ladys-international-rallying-cry-beijing-womens-rights-are-human-rights.
3. 'Sustainable Development Goals: 17 Goals to Transform our World', United Nations. https://www.un.org/en/exhibits/page/sdgs-17-goals-transform-world

1. A World for the Educated

1. UN Declaration of Human Rights, Article 26, 1948. https://www.un.org/en/udhrbook/pdf/udhr_booklet_en_web.pdf.
2. *National Family Health Survey (NFHS-5), 2019–21: India*, Vol 1, Ministry of Health and Family Welfare, Government of India. https://dhsprogram.com/pubs/pdf/FR375/FR375.pdf.
3. The Meena community are a Scheduled Tribe, traditionally considered descendants of the Rajputs, with some population historically leading semi-nomadic lives. They are found predominantly in Rajasthan and, to a lesser extent, in Punjab.
4. MGNREGA is a widely discussed and often revered social safety net—the world's largest public works programme. Legislated in 2005 as NREGA and launched in 2006, it guarantees any rural resident over the age of eighteen up to 100 days of minimum-wage employment each year. In practice, the scheme has only partially succeeded: the average number of days of work provided has plateaued at around forty-five, with wages of 255 rupees per day. Yet in 2022, the programme still employed 143 million people to work in the fields or 'create assets'—planting, ploughing, clearing weeds, cleaning drains, deepening

ponds, even building roads. In 2009, a government amendment renamed the scheme MGNREGA. Research indicates that it has increased household income by an average of 13 per cent and reduced income-based poverty by around 18 per cent. For more, see: 'MGNREGA Implementation Status', https://libtech.in/wp-content/uploads/2023/10/India_Apr-Sep_2023.pdf.

5. SIGAR Report, 'What We Need to Learn: Twenty Years of Afghanistan Reconstruction', August 2021, p. 3. https://www.sigar.mil/pdf/lessonslearned/SIGAR-21-46-LL.pdf. Accessed 23 April 2024.
6. Prior to the Taliban's first period of rule from 1996, there has been some progress under the Soviets, with girls numbering close to one-third of the school-going population in 1990. But by 2000, UNICEF reported that only 4–5 per cent of Afghan children were being educated at the primary school level. For more, see: 'The Securitization of Education in Afghanistan', EFSAS, September 2022, https://www.efsas.org/publications/articles-by-efsas/the-securitization-of-education-in-afghanistan/.
7. PTI, 'Malala slams Afghan Taliban for instituting "gender apartheid"', *The Tribune*, 13 January 2025. https://www.tribuneindia.com/news/world/malala-slams-afghan-taliban-for-instituting-gender-apartheid/. Accessed 12 October 2025.
8. Despite huge progress, India is not yet on track to eliminate the practice by 2030. One-third of child brides still live in India. This follows a pattern of 'hotspots' and over half of India's child brides can be found in just five states. For more, see: 'Ending Child Marriage: A profile of progress in India', UNICEF, 5 May 2023, https://data.unicef.org/resources/ending-child-marriage-a-profile-of-progress-in-india-2023. Accessed 5 November 2025.
9. According to a 2024 UNICEF report, child labour in India is declining, with only an estimated 0.7 per cent of children aged five to seventeen working as child labourers. Yet this still amounts to more than 1.8 million children. For more, see: 'Child Labour and Schooling in India: A Reappraisal', UNICEF Innocenti, 2024. https://www.unicef.org/innocenti/media/9356/file/UNICEF-Innocenti-Child-labour-schooling-India-Report-2024.pdf. Accessed 5 October 2025.

10. In India during the 2000s, the Sarva Shiksha Abhiyan (SSA) implemented bridge courses to address educational gaps and ensure that all children, especially those from marginalized communities, could benefit from elementary education. These bridge courses fell under the Alternative Education provision of the SSA and aimed to prepare students for formal schooling by providing them with foundational skills in reading, writing and mathematics as well as life skills. They were often designed to be flexible and adaptable to the specific needs of the students. For more, see: 'Sarva Shiksha Abhiyan: Manual for Planning and Appraisal', Ministry of Human Resource Development, Department of Education and Literacy, April 2004, https://dsel.education.gov.in/sites/default/files/2019-05/Manual_Planning_and_Apprisal.pdf.
11. A KGBV is a residential secondary school for girls run by the Ministry of Education in India. For more, visit: https://www.niepa.ac.in/KGBV/index.html.
12. 'Pukka' describes a dwelling built to be solid and permanent.
13. 'Introducing Nelson Mandela', Mandela Exhibition. https://mandelaexhibition.com/wp-content/uploads/2019/02/Mandela_EDU_Introducing-Mandela_power_point_FINAL.pdf. Accessed 10 November 2025.
14. According to UNESCO's figures for 2023, published in the 'Global Education Monitoring Report' (2025). For more details, see: 'Out-of-School Rate', UNESCO, https://education-estimates.org/out-of-school/. Accessed 1 January 2025.

2. On the Margins

1. Hans Rosling quoted in Melinda Gates, *The Moment of Lift: How Empowering Women Changes the World* (London: Bluebird, 2019), p. 240.
2. 'Economic Survey Highlights Thrust on Rural Development', Press Information Bureau, Government of India, 1 February 2023. https://www.pib.gov.in/PressReleasePage.aspx?PRID=1894901&reg=3&lang=2. Accessed 1 December 2025.
3. A block is a rural administrative unit—the subdivision of a district used for planning and development purposes.

4. 'Kutcha' means makeshift or temporary, typically describing a structure or construction such as a road.
5. An estimated 1.1 billion people were living in multidimensional poverty in 2024. India is home to the largest share, at 234 million. 'Global Multidimensional Poverty Index 2024 (MPI): Poverty Amid Conflict', Human Development Reports, 17 October 2024, https://hdr.undp.org/content/2024-global-multidimensional-poverty-index-mpi#/indicies/MPI. Accessed 1 December 2025.
6. Suresh Tendulkar, *Report of the Expert Group to Review the Methodology for Estimation of Poverty* (Government of India Planning Commission: New Delhi, 2011).
7. Oxford Poverty and Human Development Initiative (OPHI), 'Global Multidimensional Poverty Index 2021: Unmasking disparities by ethnicity, caste and gender', UNDP, p. 16, https://ophi.org.uk/sites/default/files/2024-02/GMPI_2021_Unmasking.pdf. Accessed 5 October 2025.
8. Based on data from the All India Debt and Investment Survey (AIDIS) and the Periodic Labour Force Survey (PLFS). Also, Abhishek Jha and Roshan Kishore, 'Muslims in India the Poorest Religious Group, with High Inequality and Limited Opportunities, Data Analysis Reveals', *Hindustan Times*, 5 October 2025, https://www.hindustantimes.com/india-news/muslims-in-india-the-poorest-religious-group-with-high-inequality-and-limited-opportunities-data-analysis-reveals-101688097160955.html. Accessed 5 October 2025.
9. 'Girls' education', UNICEF. https://www.unicef.org/education/girls-education. Accessed 5 October 2025.
10. 'Sakshi's story: "My parents named me *unwanted*"', *BBC News*, 24 October 2011. https://www.bbc.com/news/world-south-asia-15429531. Accessed 15 October 2025.
11. *How Many Girls Are Missing at Birth in India? Trends in Sex Ratio at Birth, 2001–2012* (United Nations Population Fund India: New Delhi, 2015). //efaidnbmnnnibpcajpcglclefindmkaj/https://india.unfpa.org/sites/default/files/pub-pdf/TrendsinSRB.pdf. Accessed 1 October 2025.
12. 'Uneven Expectations: Measuring Gender Norms to Address Children's Engagement in Unpaid Work', UNICEF, 2021. https://

data.unicef.org/resources/uneven-expectations-measuring-gender-norms-to-address-childrens-engagement-in-unpaid-work/. Accessed on 5 October 2025.

13. Studies show that 50 per cent of girls of reproductive age in India have iron deficiency anaemia compared to 23 per cent of boys. Studies have focused on the biological determinants, but this study looks at how gender norms affect anaemia in select villages in Odisha (2021). For more, see: Erica Sedlander et al, 'How gender norms affect anemia in select villages in rural Odisha, India: A qualitative study', *Science Direct*, Vol. 86, 2021. https://www.sciencedirect.com/science/article/pii/S0899900721000216. Accessed 5 October 2025.
14. The Bhil tribe are usually agriculturalists whose income is closely linked to the climate—a failed monsoon can limit their income to a single crop in a year.
15. 'Humanitarian Action for Children', UNICEF, 2023. https://www.unicef.org/media/131516/file/2023-HAC-India.pdf. Accessed 5 October 2025.
16. 'The Impact of the Tsunami on Women', Oxfam Briefing Note, Oxfam International, March 2005. https://oxfamilibrary.openrepository.com/bitstream/handle/10546/115038/bn-tsunami-impact-on-women-250305-en.pdf.
17. 'Education in Emergencies', UNICEF, https://www.unicef.org/education/emergencies. Accessed 5 October 2025.

3. Changing a School of Thought

1. An anganwadi worker, under the Integrated Child Development Services (ICDS), supports pregnant women, new mothers and children under six. For more, visit: http://wcd.delhi.gov.in/wcd/services-under-integrated-child-development-services.
2. 'Teachers in India in 2021-22: The picture from UDISE+', TISS, p. 17. https://tiss.ac.in/uploads/files/SOTTTER-23_BP1_UDISE.pdf. The study discusses how '67 per cent of all teachers in urban areas are women compared to 44 per cent in rural areas.' This paper has used UDISE 2021–22 data.
3. India's midday meal programme—the world's largest free school-feeding initiative—aims to improve nutrition and boost

school attendance by providing lunch to an estimated 120 million children each weekday in government primary and upper-primary schools. For more, visit: https://pmposhan-ams.education.gov.in/About_mdm.aspx.

4. Learning Who Should Lead

1. The centre in a village is where the government ICDS childcare programme is run.
2. 'Report on Employment and Unemployment survey 2009-10', NSSO. https://dge.gov.in/dge/sites/default/files/2022-11/EUS_2009-10.pdf. According to the report, 35 females per 1,000 in rural India (3.5 per cent) attained above secondary level of education.
3. 'Women and Men in India', Ministry of Statistics and Programme Implementation, 2016. https://mospi.gov.in/sites/default/files/reports_and_publication/statistical_publication/social_statistics/WM16Chapter3.pdf.
4. The Gram Panchayat is an elected body of village members, led by a sarpanch who becomes a government official.

5. Lessons in How to Count Girls

1. Melinda Gates, *The Moment of Lift: How Empowering Women Changes the World* (Flatiron Books: London, 2019), p. 240.
2. Educate Girls, 'Project Completion Report', January 2010, p. 4, https://www.educategirls.ngo/wp-content/uploads/2022/10/Proof-of-Concept.pdf.
3. 'The Global Gender Gap Report', World Economic Forum Geneva, Switzerland, 2006. https://www3.weforum.org/docs/WEF_GenderGap_Report_2006.pdf
4. This estimate is based on the 2011 Census and the Socio-Economic Caste survey. For more, visit: https://secc.dord.gov.in/.
5. These figures come from the 2001 Census as cited in Educate Girls, 'Project Completion Report', 2010, p. 8.
6. 'National Family Health Survey NFHS–3, 2005–2006 NFHS-3', Ministry of Health and Family Welfare, September 2007, p. 208. https://dhsprogram.com/pubs/pdf/frind3/frind3-vol1andvol2.pdf.
7. Ibid, p. 166.

8. Educate Girls, 'Project Completion Report', 2010. https://www.educategirls.ngo/wp-content/uploads/2022/10/Proof-of-Concept.pdf. Accessed 5 October 2025.
9. Dr Santanu Bhattacharya, 'Automated Systems to Solve India's $10B+ Addressing Problem', *Medium*, 20 January 2019, https://santanub.medium.com/automated-systems-to-solve-indias-10b-addressing-problem-9063190921ef. Accessed 1 October 2025.

6. The Making of a Movement

1. 'Paying the Price: The Economic Cost of Failing to Educate Girls', Plan International, 2008, p. 9, https://resourcecentre.savethechildren.net/pdf/4744.pdf. Accessed 1 February 2025.
2. Kusum Kali Pal et al, 'Global Gender Gap Report 2024', World Economic Forum, 11 June 2024. https://www.weforum.org/publications/global-gender-gap-report-202. Accessed 1 February 2025.
3. Project Completion Report, Educate Girls, 2010.
4. As reported in 2009, the Telecom Regulatory Authority of India (TRIA) said that mobile penetration in rural areas is less than 13 per cent, compared with 73 per cent in urban areas. Charles Arthur, 'Mobile Phone Growth in India Slows as Saturation Point Nears', *The Guardian*, 22 January 2009. https://www.theguardian.com/technology/2009/jan/22/mobile-phones-india-telecoms. Accessed 5 October 2025.
5. *The Tree* (2010), Times of India - Lead India. https://www.youtube.com/watch?v=c9L3ReT7UuQ.

7. Moving at Speed

1. Alice Calaprice, ed., *The Ultimate Quotable Einstein* (Princeton, NJ: Princeton University Press, 2010).
2. MGNREGA, 'MGNREGA Implementation Status'.
3. For more information on the Development Impact Bond, see IDinsight, 'Educate Girls Development Impact Bond Final Evaluation Report', 10 June 2018. https://www.educategirls.ngo/wp-content/uploads/2022/10/ID_Insight_2018_Educate_Girls_Development_Impact_Bond_-_Final_Evaluation_Report.pdf.

4. 'Mission with a Vision, Annual Report 2016–2017', Ministry of Human Resource Development. https://www.education.gov.in/sites/upload_files/mhrd/files/document-reports/HRD%20AR%202016-17%20SE.pdf.

8. The Multiplier Effect

1. Lawrence H. Summers, 'Investing in All the People: Educating Women in Developing Countries', Economic Development Institute of the World Bank, 1994. https://documents1.worldbank.org/curated/en/492291468765047177/pdf/multi-page.pdf.
2. Keiron Boyle, 'What the search for a social unicorn tells us about scaling impact', *LSE*, Marshall Institute, 1 April 2025. https://blogs.lse.ac.uk/socialbusinesshub/2025/04/01/what-the-search-for-a-social-unicorn-tells-us-about-scaling-impact/.
3. 'Social Unicorn, Safeena Husain receives Honorary Doctorate from LSE for Championing Girls' Education in India', 100x Impact, 6 June 2024. https://www.100ximpact.org/resources/social-unicorn-safeena-husain-receives-honorary-doctorate-from-london-school-of-economics-for-championing-girls-education-in-india.
4. An upsarpanch is a member of a gram panchayat, the village-level constitutional body of local self-government. The sarpanch is the main decision-maker.
5. Ministry of Panchayat Raj, Government of India archives. https://archive.ph/20140211173048/http://panchayat.nic.in/brgf/.
6. Gene B. Sperling and Rebecca Winthrop, *What Works in Girls' Education* (Brookings Institution Press: USA, p. 25. https://www.brookings.edu/wp-content/uploads/2016/07/What-Works-in-Girls-Educationlowres.pdf. (Please see: G. Psacharopoulos's calculations in the report).
7. D. Dollar and Roberta Garri, 'Gender Inequality, Income and Growth: Are Good Times Good for Women', *Working Paper 1 for Policy Research Report on Gender and Development* (Washington: World Bank, 1999).
8. 'The Case for Holistic Investment in Girls', Plan International and Citi Global, 2020. https://plan-international.org/

uploads/2021/12/report_citi_gps_girls_in_the_economy_submitted.pdf.

9. Ibid.
10. Emmanuela Gakidou, et al., 'Increased Educational Attainment and Its Effect on Child Mortality in 175 Countries between 1970 and 2009: A Systematic Analysis', *Lancet* 376, no. 9745 (2010): 959–74.

    Also, Also, Sperling and Winthrop, *What Works in Girls' Education*, p. 29.
11. A study of child mortality in 175 countries from 1970 to 2009 found that increases in women's education were responsible for more than half the reduction in under-five child mortality. That's 4.2 million lives saved because of girls' education. Meeting the SDG target for under-five mortality could save 11 million lives by 2030. Emmanuela Gakidou, et al., 'Increased Educational Attainment and Its Effect on Child Mortality in 175 Countries between 1970 and 2009: A Systematic Analysis', *Lancet* 376, no. 9745 (2010): 959–74.

    Also, Also, Sperling and Winthrop, *What Works in Girls' Education*, p. 29.
12. 'Her Education Our Future: The Latest Facts on Gender Equality in Education', UNESCO, 2020. https://reliefweb.int/report/world/hereducationourfuture-latest-facts-gender-equality-education. Accessed 5 October 2025.
13. Ibid.
14. Sperling and Winthrop, *What Works in Girls' Education*, pp. 17–19.
15. 'Girls' Education and Women's Equality: How to Get More out of the World's Most Promising Investment', Center for Global Development (CGD), 2022, p. 28. Based on a review of eighty-nine rigorous studies, the link has been made between more and better education and improved health outcomes.
16. UNESCO has shown that universal primary education for girls would reduce child mortality by 15 per cent and universal secondary education would reduce it by 49 per cent. 'Teaching and Learning: Achieving Quality for All—EFA Global Monitoring Report 2013–14', UNESCO. https://gsdrc.org/

document-library/20134-education-for-all-global-monitoring-report-teaching-and-learning-achieving-quality-for-all/.
Also, 'Progress for Children: Achieving the MDGs with Equity', UNICEF. https://ses.sp.bvs.br/local/File/Progress%20for%20Children_Achieving%20the%20MDGs%20with%20Equity.pdf.
Also Also, Also, Sperling and Winthrop, *What Works in Girls' Education*, p. 30.

17. 'Gender gap in primary, secondary and tertiary education, World', Our World in Data. https://ourworldindata.org/grapher/gender-gap-education-levels. Accessed 1 October 2025. (Note: figures for secondary education are not available at this source.)
18. Sperling and Winthrop, *What Works in Girls' Education*, p. 57. Also, S. Bhalotra, I. Clots-Figueras and L. Iyer, *Women's Political Participation and the Female–Male Literacy Differential in India, Background Paper Commissioned for EFA, Global Monitoring Report*, 2013–14 (Paris: UNESCO, 2013).
19. Ibid.
Also, A. Basu and E.M. King, *Does Education Promote Growth and Democracy: Some Evidence from East Asia and Latin America* (Washington: World Bank, 2001).
20. R. Chattopadhyay and E. Duflo, 'Women as Policy Makers, Evidence from a Randomized Policy Experiment in India', *Econometrica*, Volume 72, no. 5 (September 2004): 1409–43. https://economics.mit.edu/sites/default/files/2022-08/Women%20as%20Policy%20Makers%20Evidence%20from%20a%20Randomized.pdf.
Also, Sperling and Winthrop, *What Works in Girls' Education*.
21. 'Violence and harassment in the world of work: A guide on Convention No. 190 and Recommendation No. 206', International Labour Organization, 2021. https://www.ilo.org/sites/default/files/wcmsp5/groups/public/@dgreports/@gender/documents/publication/wcms_814507.pdf.
22. P.K.V. Kishan, 'Is the Past Still Holding Us Back? A Study on Intergenerational Education Mobility in India', IIM Ahmedabad, January 2018. https://www.iima.ac.in/sites/default/files/rnpfiles/20034924042018-01-03.pdf.

23. John Doerr, *Speed & Scale: An Action Plan for Solving our Climate Crisis Now* (Penguin Business: USA, 2021).
24. Sperling and Winthrop, *What Works in Girls' Education*, p. 60.
25. E. Streissnig, W. Lutz and A. Patt, 'Effects of Educational Attainment on Climate Risk Vulnerability', *Ecology and Society*, Volume 18, no. 1 (2013): 16. http://www.jstor.org/stable/26269263.
26. A. Namasivayam, A. Graves, C. Kwauk and C. Frischmann, 'Drawdown's Health and Education Solution', Project Drawdown 2022. https://drawdown.org/sites/default/files/Drawdown-Solutions-Policy-Brief-Health-and-Education.pdf.
27. In 2021, G7 leaders set goals to improve girls' education in low- and lower-middle-income countries by 2026: 40 million more girls in school and 20 million more girls reading by age ten. UN Girls' Education Initiative, https://www.ungei.org/publication/g7-global-objectives-girls-education. Educate Girls is featured on p. 52 of the baseline report.

9. The Meaning of an Education

1. According to the India Human Development Survey conducted in 2017, cited here: Lavanya Garg, '80 per cent Indian women need permission to visit health centre, 5 per cent have sole control over choice of husband', *Scroll*, 14 February 2017. https://scroll.in/article/829205/80-indian-women-need-permission-to-visit-health-centre-5-have-sole-control-over-choice-of-husband.
2. Analysis for Educate Girls from India Human Development Survey–II, 2011–12. https://ihds.umd.edu/data/ihds-2.

Conclusion

1. Ministry of Education, 'UDISE+ Report 2024–2025'. https://www.education.gov.in/sites/upload_files/mhrd/files/statistics-new/UDISE%2BReport%202024-25%20-%20NEP%20Structure.pdf.
2. 'Periodic Labour Force Survey (PLFS), Key Employment Unemployment Indicators for (January 2024–December 2024)', Periodic Labour Force Survey, , https://microdata.gov.in/NADA/index.php/catalog/254.
3. UDISE+ Report 2024–2025.

About the Author

Safeena Husain has worked extensively with rural and urban underserved communities in South America, Africa and Asia. Armed with a degree from London School of Economics, Husain first worked in a start-up in Silicon Valley, USA. She soon switched gears to lead a US-based non-profit organization for seven years. In 2004, she returned to India to take on an issue close to her heart and launched Educate Girls in 2007. She has shepherded the organization through dramatic growth since then. In 2025, Educate Girls became the first Indian organization to win the Ramon Magsaysay Award.

HarperCollins *Publishers* India

At HarperCollins India, we believe in telling the best stories and finding the widest readership for our books in every format possible. We started publishing in 1992; a great deal has changed since then, but what has remained constant is the passion with which our authors write their books, the love with which readers receive them, and the sheer joy and excitement that we as publishers feel in being a part of the publishing process.

Over the years, we've had the pleasure of publishing some of the finest writing from the subcontinent and around the world, including several award-winning titles and some of the biggest bestsellers in India's publishing history. But nothing has meant more to us than the fact that millions of people have read the books we published, and that somewhere, a book of ours might have made a difference.

As we look to the future, we go back to that one word—a word which has been a driving force for us all these years.

Read.

Harper Collins · Harper Sport · HARPER FICTION · HARPER NON-FICTION · हार्पर हिन्दी

HARPER LEARNING · HARPER VANTAGE · HCCB HARPERCOLLINS CHILDREN'S BOOKS · 4th · HARPER PERENNIAL

HARPER DESIGN · BOOKTOPUS · HARPER BUSINESS